THE VIN
OF ENGLAN

2005 GUIDE

THE **WINE** GUILD

OF THE UNITED KINGDOM

First Published in Great Britain in 2005 by

THE WINE GUILD
OF THE UNITED KINGDOM
Christmas Cottage, North Street,
Petworth, West Sussex, GU28 0DF

Edited by
Colin Vaughan
Tim Hazell
Michael Hildesley

The publishers and Editors wish to acknowledge with thanks the support received from English Wine Producers and the United Kingdom Vineyards Association in the production of this Guide.

Grateful thanks are also given to Food from Britain for its generous sponsorship.

ISBN 0-9550300-0-5

Designed and Printed in Great Britain by
OAK DESIGN AND PRINT
info@oakdp.co.uk

Sponsored by

FOOD *from* Britain

Cover photo: Three Choirs Vineyard.

THE WINE GUILD

OF THE UNITED KINGDOM

It is with great pleasure that the Wine Guild of the United Kingdom offers you this Official Guide to the Vineyards of England and Wales.

It would not surprise our Roman or Mediaeval forebears to know that wine is produced here, but they would be astounded by the variety and quality of the wines. Variety, because our enthusiastic growers are still perfecting the range of varieties to best suit British conditions, which vary enormously across the country. Quality, because of the investment in state-of-the-art equipment and adoption of the latest ideas, training and best practices in both vineyard husbandry and winery management – but also because of the determination of the whole industry to seek continual improvement wherever and whenever possible.

At Beaulieu we are proud to have been in the forefront of the twentieth century new wave of English wine producers, and I am personally delighted to have witnessed the enormous strides taken in such a relatively brief time. When we planted our vineyard in 1959, albeit on the site of the Beaulieu monastic vineyard, few of us would have thought we would live to see over 300 vineyards in this country, and nearly half of those commercial.

I am also delighted that so many producers welcome visitors to their vineyards and are happy to explain, guide and tutor, so that we may all improve our knowledge and understanding of the fascinating culture which is the wine industry. This lies at the heart of our mission as a Wine Guild, and our hope is that this guide will not only be of use to those already interested in English and Welsh wines, but will help introduce many more to the pleasures of wine generally, and of these wines in particular.

We are grateful to the United Kingdom Vineyards Association, the English Wine Producers and Food for Britain for their enthusiastic support

Montagu of Beaulieu
CHANCELLOR
Wine Guild of the United Kingdom

OBJECTIVES OF THE WINE GUILD

The Wine Guild is a society of wine lovers whose purpose is to communicate the appreciation of wine – aesthetic and pleasurable – to others and to encourage greater knowledge. It fosters good fellowship amongst its members, who are drawn from the wine production industry, wine trade, hospitality industry and individual wine lovers.

The Guild supports the revival of English and Welsh wine growing and is a member of the Federation Internationale des Confreries Bachiques.

In its ceremony the Guild reflects the tradition of craft guilds of mediaeval Europe but it is modern in the exercise of its aims.

It has social and educational roles. Socially it has an active programme of events including banquets as well as tutored and informal tastings. A foreign tour to a wine growing region is organised every second year and is very popular.

Educationally, through its charitable trust, it promotes scholarships for the study of wine within the wine, hotel and catering trade.

If you would like to know more contact:

The Secretary
The Wine Guild of the United Kingdom
North Street
Petworth
West Sussex
GU28 0DF

CONTENTS

INTRODUCTION

Colin Vaughan, Tim Hazell and Mike Hildesley

Anyone who has yet to visit a vineyard has missed out on one of the great pleasures in this life: to see the carefully trained, lovingly tended vines is to begin to appreciate the full wonder of the winegrower's task. It requires such skill and patience to work with Nature, to avoid frost and to capture the sunshine available, to fight off mildews and pests, and bring them forth the best that each year's weather and the local 'terroir' will permit. Then follows the crucial decision as to when to harvest, to capture the moment when ripeness and acidity will give the best possible chance for the winemaker to show his or her skills to best advantage.

As Julia Trustram Eve points out in her article, you do not have to cross the Channel to enjoy this experience: there are over 300 active vineyards across the breadth of England and Wales, as far north as Yorkshire (and maybe, with global warming, soon further north), of which we list nearly 150, at many of which you can enjoy a whole range of vineyard experiences. Some specifically cater for the tourist, with a wide range of attractions. Others may offer no more than a chance to walk in the vineyard and taste some wines, hopefully encouraging you to buy some to enjoy at home with friends or family. All those we have visited have afforded us a truly warm welcome.

Whether you are contemplating a day trip, or are looking for a week-end or short stay away, or even as a base for a longer holiday, you will find something in this Guide to give purpose to your trip into the countryside – and many of these vineyards nestle among the more attractive valleys and countryside to be found in these islands. You will find details of the accommodation and other facilities available at those vineyards in the main listing.

Don't worry if you are not a 'wine expert': what matters most is your own taste and what you like – and what better way to judge that than by going and tasting for yourself! Helpfully, wines now have to conform to certain labelling laws, as is more fully explained in the article on page 69 – but in short, 'Quality' now means quality, and 'Regional' is a step above 'Table wine'.

Want to learn more about wine? Why not look out for those vineyards which offer guided tours and tastings – some even offer 'Wine Experience' packages (a wonderful birthday or anniversary gift idea!) with tutoring and maybe a meal with wine – and perhaps somewhere to stay and sleep it off if you think you might get too interested!

English and Welsh wines have come a long way in the last couple of decades: you may not find every English (or French or Australian) wine to your taste, but we can assure you that, out there waiting to be discovered are English and Welsh wines which are winning international competitions, and there is something for almost every taste.

We hope you will have as much pleasure using this Guide as we have had bringing it together!

A TASTING OF ENGLISH AND WELSH WINES

Maggie McNie MW

In preparation for this Guide, a Panel of six people, led by Maggie McNie MW and Richard Bampfield MW, tasted more than eighty wines over two days. They were not asked to judge the wines or rank them competitively (there are numerous regional, national and international competitions which do that), but rather to assess their characteristics in order to help readers in their own expectations as to what they may find as they explore the vineyards listed.

Overall impressions:

All the members of the Panel were pleasantly surprised by the high quality of a large number of the wines offered for tasting, as well as by the wide range of styles offered: sparkling and still; red, white and rosé; blended or single varietal; conventional and late harvested – and even a rarity for this country, some 'old vine' production. We were struck that here is a youthful, vibrant and exciting industry, and many of the wines were clearly well and lovingly made. How is it that such a relatively small industry can produce such good quality over such a wide variety?

A little historical perspective may help:

Vineyards: although there is evidence of some wine production, as far back as the Romans, the modern wine industry's roots are little more than fifty years old, starting with three experimental plantings, at Hambledon, Horam Manor and then Beaulieu. Once it was demonstrated that wine could be made and sold commercially in England and Wales, others began to join in and the first growers' associations (first Wales and then England!) were formed in the 1960's. The very hot summer of 1976 heralded a third wave of new plantings, and, while many small vineyards may have come and gone, grubbed up for economic reasons, the overall number of vineyards has continued to grow, so that today there are estimated to be over 300, with about 200 producing wine for sale, albeit some in very small quantities and some growing grapes for other wine makers.

Winemaking: while all this was going on, there were significant developments in winemaking, notably the application of science in many New World countries, and the vastly improved training of a younger generation of winemakers, well able to take advantage of new technologies.

Early wine-making in this country had looked to Germany as having the closest climate, and much help came from Germany as did many of the varieties planted: the style of wine was therefore Germanic – soft, fruity and with obvious residual sugar, as had been very popular for some decades (given the difficulty of achieving full ripeness, some added sugar was permitted, as in Germany). But as, for reasons too complex to go into here, the British consumer began to ask for drier wines to drink with meals, and as many New World producers in Australia, California, Chile and New Zealand showed the desirability of judicious use of oak in wine production, so producers here have looked at the possibility of not only making drier styles of wine, but also of making red wines, sparkling wines and even, in favourable years, some fine dessert wines.

Professionalism is evident, if not in all aspects everywhere, certainly in many aspects in most places: in the choice of wine-making equipment, in the care taken in the vineyard as well as the winery, as well as in respect for the 'terroir', which varies enormously across this small country, in terms of geology, prevailing weather and microclimatic features.

Why such variety of wines and styles?

To quote Sir Winston Churchill, we are today not at the beginning of the end, but we may be at the end of the beginning. We have seen a small band of enthusiastic experimenters becoming a relatively well established if still small industry, and that despite minimal official support or assistance, unlike most other wine producing nations. But thirty years is little or no time in the context of most producing regions: it takes three years from planting to first production, and you only get one chance each year to try some new method in the vineyard or winery – consider how many times a chef may experiment with a dish before presenting it to his or her public and you may begin to understand the winemaker's dilemma. To grub up one set of vines and replant another variety is a minimum five year decision – so it is not surprising that some sought safety in variety, thereby also reducing the risk of a catastrophic harvest on one particular variety. For many, variety and the chance to try something new is part of the reason they are in this business – if it was an easy life they were after, they would hardly choose this particular field!

What should you expect?

Still Whites: This tasting was typical of what you might expect in visiting the vineyards: over half the wines presented were still white wines, and of these some half were blends and the rest were selected single varietals: the names -for instance, Bacchus, Ortega, Madeleine Angevine, Kerner and Reichensteiner – may not be as familiar as Chardonnay or Sauvignon Blanc, but they are for the most part dry, aromatic wines, offering crispness and flavour, even a little spiciness in some cases. Typically quite subtle and delicate in flavour, you may be surprised to find how well made and structured many of these white wines are. With a good backbone of acidity and alcohol giving them balance, they go well with food as well as on their own – and some offer good potential for ageing, when additional, more honeyed flavours can appear, although the wine will remain dry.

A few wines did disappoint, but mostly they were of a consistently high standard and a handful stood out as of international standing. Many of the blends are clearly aimed to be drunk with food, but will equally provide a summer aperitif, while the single varietal wines are far more than an education in the characteristics of each variety, and offer some fine wines and interesting flavours. Chapel Down, Denbies and Three Choirs offer a large range, but many smaller producers also offer three, four or more wines – and to pick out a few names would be invidious: we hope you will explore for yourself and find what you like!

Rosés: The surprise of the tasting was the quality of the rosé wines – all of them were of a high standard and in this area English and Welsh wines are in at the beginning of the renaissance for rosé wines: forget the mass produced brand familiar to most of us, and be prepared to back your own – and our – judgement that here are wines well worth having chilled on a warm summer's evening! If you are anywhere near Cardiff, why not try a bottle of Cariad?

Sparkling wines: here we must draw a distinction between those who have set out so successfully to produce a rival to Champagne, such as Ridgeview and Nyetimber, using the traditional varieties as well as the same production method (justifiably, since the English Mr Merret described this method before Dom Perignon began his famous work), and the large range of other sparkling wines, typically using more aromatic varieties, many of which are delicious if you are not prejudicing your taste-buds with an expectation of a champagne taste. Indeed, the Panel, as an aside, mentioned its belief that an attractive tank fermented sparkling wine should be a real option for many producers in this country and might be considerably more economic than using the secondary bottle fermentation on the lees of the champagne method, which in any case tends to kill the aromatic flavours.

Red wines: many producers are now including red wines, often blended, in their range, but in comparison with most of the white wines the learning curve is, in truth, only just beginning. Widest planted is the relatively international Pinot Noir (also used in some sparkling wines), but there are some interesting and less familiar new varieties, such as Dornfelder which gives spectacular colour and powerful fruit even in a cooler climate and goes well with oak, (Biddenden offers a single varietal Dornfelder and Bookers a Rondo/Dornfelder blend), as well as the more widely planted Rondo and Regent varieties. Red wines are much more dependent on full ripeness to achieve a well balanced wine, and there were some good examples - happily we can expect even more and better red wine production, especially if the weather continues to warm, as growers and winemakers learn by their own experience as well as from other cooler climate producers.

Specialist late harvest, dessert and old vine wines: none of these are widely available, but if you should spot one, it is normally worth the extra cost to try a bottle, and certainly worth tasting if you are given the chance. As the name suggests, late harvest means that the grapes have been left on the vines, often into late October or November, and if the grapes remain free of undesirable rot and other blights, and have not been eaten by hungry birds, the result is usually a riper and more concentrated but certainly smaller harvest. The wine may consequently be off-dry or even sweet, but the flavours will be enhanced. Likewise, if the grapes have been attacked by botrytis cinerea ('Noble Rot'), which certainly does not happen every year, careful harvesting can result in spectacular dessert wines – and these can age well, as a recent bottle of 1992 botrytis affected Optima showed.

Less obviously special, but always worth looking out for, are wines made from old vines: these should be at least twenty-five years old, and the result is often a more concentrated flavour resulting from deeper penetrating roots (terroir) and more modest levels of production per vine. An example is Astley's Old Kerner, and their Madeleine Angevine vines are mostly similarly aged.

Regional differences: based on this tasting it is hard to say there are any major differences ascribable to region – more important are vineyard, variety and winemaker. Certainly the differences would not have us sending readers across the country in search of a regional style. That said, the Welsh samples had a delicate crispness and flavour whereas those from the South-West tended to be a little richer. The Wessex wines tended to be very dry in style, with the most successful showing the high alcohol necessary to achieve good balance. Mercian and Midlands wines offered great variety, and a couple of special samples showed the ageing potential of some of these white wines. The South-East had a fine range of quality wines, and is for the moment the outstanding area for sparkling wines, with East Anglia producing a mainly crisp, dry style. But in each and every area you will find exceptions.

Ageing potential: the long, slow ripening of the grapes in this country not only produces fine flavours but also high acidity, and although many of the wines can seem light, crisp and designed for early drinking, the best of them can and do age well and develop wonderful flavours if they are cellared properly. It is a fallacy that English and Welsh wines need to be drunk very young to show at their best – but you would be advised to taste carefully yourself, or seek the producer's advice, before laying down these wines in quantity. We can say that some old 'forgotten' bottles have tasted wonderful, and made certain Panel members wish they had not drunk so many bottles of some wines so young, while the ten and twenty year old wines we were able to include in this tasting certainly attested to the ageing potential!

The ageing potential of the red wines is hard to judge as yet: the structure is there, but whether the fruit will survive long enough is doubtful in many cases: over-aged cool climate pinot noir can become thin and watery, but some producers are clearly intent on producing a fuller style of red wine which may age five or more years and it might be worth a small experiment of your own, if you have the cellar space.

Vintages: you will not often find still wines with more than one or two vintages available, and during the currency of this guide we anticipate that you will mainly find 2004 vintage wines with some 2003's. Given the hot summer in 2003 many predicted a wonderful vintage for English and Welsh wines – and certainly there was excellent ripeness. However, in many instances acidity levels were lower than usual, leading to less structured white wines and consequently, as a general rule, we would suggest that 2003 wines should be consumed sooner rather than be cellared for a long time, while early indications are that the 2004 vintage may actually prove the better all round vintage for white wines in the longer term. The 2003 reds should have benefited from the additional ripeness. A few 1996 sparkling wines may still be available and certainly 1998 is around for those seeking a vintage Champagne character, albeit at similar prices.

Conclusion: we anticipate that over the next decade and more, there will be a gradual evolution of the industry towards certain varieties and styles, albeit with plenty of scope for individual producers. Much will depend on the weather, on changes in consumer patterns and on continuing support for our wine producers, but our feeling is that we are blessed with an enthusiastic, youthful and professional industry which is more than deserving of our attention, and where the diligent searcher will be more than rewarded for his or her efforts! Our hope is that this Guide will be your companion on your journey.

Plumpton College

PLUMPTON COLLEGE
Ditchling Road, Plumpton, Nr Lewes,
East Sussex BN7 3AE,
Telephone: 01273 890454
Web: www.plumpton.co.uk
E-mail: enquiries@plumpton.co.uk

A considerable part of the increasingly fresh and very professional approach to wine production in this country is due to the education affered by Plumpton College and the courses they have specifically designed.

Plumpton College is situated near Brighton in Sussex, in the heart of the South of England. Originally established in 1926 as the county's agricultural college, we are now an independent corporation with charitable status. There are around 600 full-time and 1000 part-time students studying courses including Farming, Forestry, Horticulture, Agricultural Mechanics and, uniquely within the U.K., Wine Studies for which it is a designated centre of excellence.

The Wine Studies courses are developing rapidly and cover wine making, vine growing and the Intermediate, Advanced and Diploma qualifications of the Wine and Spirits Education Trust (WSET). Courses range from amateur part-time through 2 year Foundation degrees to 3 year full-time undergraduate degrees, (in partnership with the University of Brighton) in Wine Production (FdSc), Wine Business (FdA) and Bsc (Hons) Viticulture & Oenology.

The **Foundation Degree in Wine Business** course has been designed specifically for students wishing to enter the wine trade or start their own wine-related business. The course focuses on marketing, the wine trade and business management, plus modules that correspond to the WSET Diploma syllabus.

The two-year full-time **Foundation Degree in Wine Production** programme has a strong practical bias and involves students in producing Plumpton College's award winning wine using the College's well-equipped commercial vineyard and purpose built winery.

The **BSc (Hons) Viticulture & Oenology** covers wine production and aspects of related biological sciences in considerable depth. Students also complete a major undergraduate research project. The course is studied over three years, with all final year students completing a vintage in a commercial winery. Successful graduates gain an internationally-recognised qualification.

For more information, see www.plumpton.ac.uk or contact chris.foss@plumpton.ac.uk (for the production course) ruth.hancock@plumpton.ac.uk (for the wine business course) and marianne.mckay@plumpton.ac.uk (for the BSc (Hons) Viticulture &Oenology course.

Plumpton manages a 15 acre vineyard and its own winery, providing award-winning wines: three white (dry, medium dry and fumé), one rosé and one red wine – you are welcome to visit and try them.

MAIN GRAPE VARIETIES USED IN U.K.

Auxerrois It is valued for its low acidity and is extensively planted in Alsace. It produces exciting and long lasting wines if yields are kept low. It adds 'body' to blended wines.

Bacchus Its grapes have a strong and distinctive flavour, with high sugar content. It is regularly made into a single varietal wine and although common in Germany it is also very successful in this country. Prone to stem necrosis.

Chardonnay It used to be thought that this classic variety would not succeed in our conditions. This is far from true. It is now grown largely as a fundamental ingredient of the finest sparkling wines.

Dornfelder The product of a long process of vine breeding this vine was created in 1956. The wine is notable for its colour and good acidity and prospers in this country. It is one of the grapes which demonstrates that good red wine can be made in the U.K.

Faberrebe These vines are traditional in style and are not extensively planted in this country but seem to blend well with Muller Thurgau. It develops good must weight and, in Germany, can qualify for 'spätlese' status.

Fruhburgunder There are only very small plantings of this variety. It is early ripening but may not welcome our climate. It produces very light red wines.

Huxelrebe Has a rather 'muscat' style and is a very heavy producer. It needs careful management and can be used for dessert wines because of its susceptibility to 'noble rot'. It has a high natural acidity and strong aromas of elderflowers.

Kerner Bred in 1969 this is a very successful grape. It ripens reliably and produces excellent fruit. It has a style similar to Reisling and is very popular in Germany. It may well have a good future in England. A variant, 'Kernling' ripens earlier than Kerner but produces virtually identical grapes. They both need very careful canopy management.

Madeleine Angevine A vigorous vine prone to attack by wasps. Designed for northern planting, it flowers late and ripens very early. It is useful for blending since it ages well and gives sublety to other grapes in blended wines.

MAIN GRAPE VARIETIES USED IN U.K.

Continued

Muller Thurgau	The main grape in Liebfraumilch. This grape was among the first planted in the U.K when grape growing resumed. It is now less popular being seen as a producer of unstylish wines. It was used in Germany to restore the fortunes of their vineyards after the war but is now seen as bland. It is popular in central and eastern Europe. Our climate is possibly not ideal.
Ortega	This vine suits our climate and is planted extensively. It produces very full flavours. It is a cross between Muller Thurgau and Seigerrebe. It is prone to disease.
Phoenix	This is a recent cross between Bacchus and Villard Blanc. It is a hybrid and has some disease resistance. It has low acidity and high sugar levels but there is a little experience as to how it will develop in this country.
Pinot Blanc	This is a mutation of Pinot Gris (see below). There are various strains of this grape. The wine has a strong nose and, where planted, seems to ripen its fruit well and produces wine with good fruit flavours. It crops heavily in most years.
Pinot Gris	Widely grown in France, Germany, Italy and Switzerland and known by various names including Rulander, Tokay, Malvoisie and Pinot Beurot. It can produce good deep red wines or attractive aromatic white wines. In Germany it reaches high levels of both crop and sugar in favoured locations.
Pinot Meunier	A black grape now planted in this country as an essential constituent of the finest sparkling wines, with Chardonnay and Pinot Noir. It is rarely made as a single varietal either in this country or in other wine regions of the world.
Pinot Noir	This grape can make white wine, or if the must is left in contact with the skins, a deep red wine. It is the classic grape for red burgundies but is also an important element of sparkling wines in England. It is at home in the English climate and some good red wines have been made with this grape.
Regent	A hybrid grape producing red wine. It is disease resistant, has low acidity, high sugar levels and good yields.

Reichensteiner This vine performs reliably in this country producing loose bunches of early ripening grapes. It is reliable but a little bland and is often used for blending having good sugar levels. It is one of the most popular grapes in this country, and produces heavily.

Rondo A red grape, this hybrid vine has very different parentage from Regent but some of the characteristics. It is becoming more popular in this country having good colour and style and overtones of classic red varieties.

Rulander The German name for Pinot Gris.

Schonburger This grape has been very successful in the U.K producing white wines with low acidity but high sugar levels. It was bred in 1979 and its wines are distinctive, full-bodied and delicately flavoured. It is popular in this country although lacking disease resistance.

Seyval Blanc A hybrid vine with excellent disease resistance. It is widely grown and crops heavily in this country and is often used for blending. It ages well in oak barrels and can be used for still or sparkling wines.

Siegerrebe Some commentators are scathing about this grape. One of its parents was the famously spicy Gerwurtztraminer grape. It ripens sometimes to excessive levels and has a very dominating flavour. It can be grown in this country and is used to bolster blended wines. A few growers use it as a varietal in its own right – some for late harvest and dessert wines.

Triomphe d'Alsace A red grape which was initially popular in this country. It yields well and ripens early but it has low disease resistance. It has low acidity and high sugar levels and may be superseded by other more recently bred vines.

Wurzer This vine is a crossing of Muller-Thurgau and Gewurtztraminer dating from the 1930's. It is not widely planted. It does not carry a heavy crop but has strong if somewhat overpowering flavours. It has low disease resistance.

Other Varieties There are at least 20 other varieties of which most are experimental and the list of vines permitted for classified production is subject to variation year by year.

VINEYARDS

ASTLEY VINEYARDS

ASTLEY VINEYARDS
Astley, Stourport-on-Severn
Worcs. DY13 0RU
Telephone: 01299 822907

Owners: Janet Baldwin and Jonty Daniels
Winemaker: : Martin Fowke. Wines made off site at Three Choirs under Owners' direction.

VINEYARD

Established mid-1970's by Michael and Betty Bache, this is one of the longer lasting small (5acres) commercial vineyards – and deservedly so. When it started it could claim to be the most northerly in the world, but since the first significant production in 1983 it has consistently won awards in every year – due to its devotion to quality, policy of low yields (under 3 tons/acre), concentration on terroir (site and varietal characteristics) and using best modern vineyard and wine-making practices. The soil is Triassic Red sandstone and it overlooks the Severn Valley with its micro-climate. 'Integrated Pest Control' is used (minimal non-organic intervention).

VARIETIES

Old vines: Kerner, Madeleine Angevine. Others: Siegerrebe (esp. for late harvest), Phoenix and various small parcels, some experimental.

FACILITIES AND TOURS

Free entry to enjoy the surroundings and explore the vineyard in its idyllic, peaceful setting, rich in bird and wildlife. Tastings and sales. Informal guided tours can be arranged for groups of 12-20, by appointment. Self-catering holiday apartment available. Open: Mon/Thurs/Fri/Sat l0am-5pm. Sun 12 noon-5pm. Closed Tue/Wed.

WINES

Vary by vintage, but typically include a dry white blend, Kerner from Old Vines, Madeleine Angevine, and, when possible, Late Harvest Siegerrebe. All Astley wines are English Quality Wine status, many have ageing potential, and three current wines for sale have received coveted IWSC awards. The vineyard has won over 100 awards since 1984 and is recommended in Rick Stein's guide.

SALES

90% direct sales from vineyard. Distributors Evertons, Churchills, and seek out these wines at the '77' Wine Bar in Hampstead.

DIRECTIONS

Off B4196 between Holt Heath (on A443 north from Worcester) and Stourport-on-Severn; the vineyard is well signed within Astley

BEAULIEU VINEYARD

BEAULIEU VINEYARD
John Montagu Building
Beaulieu
Hants SO42 7ZN
Telephone: 01590 614625

Owner: Lord Montagu of Beaulieu
Manager: S.N. Edmondson
Mobile: 07818454507
E-mail: neil.edmondson@beaulieu.co.uk

Winemakers:
White: Roger Marchbank, Setley Ridge Vineyard
Sparkling: Vince Gower, Valley Vineyard

VINEYARD

The soil is a clay-loam sloping to the south east. The 6.4 acre vineyard is only 50ft above sea level so the micro-climate is very suitable. The tradition of vines at Beaulieu was established by Cistercian monks in the 13th century and revived by Colonel and Mrs Gore-Brown in 1959 one of the three founders of the modern industry. The vineyard forms part of the complex at the National Motor Museum.

VINES

About 40% Bacchus, 24% Muller-Thurgau, 14% Reichensteiner and Huxelrebe with 8% Seyval Blanc. The planting is intended to produce dry and medium white wines and sparkling wines.

TOURS AND FACILITIES

Unlike most vineyards in the guide this is part of a major entertainment facility namely Beaulieu Motor Museum and the rest of the Beaulieu Estate.

BIDDENDEN VINEYARDS

BIDDENDEN VINEYARDS
Little Whatmans, Gribble Bridge Lane,
Biddenden, Kent. TN27 8DF.
Telephone: 01580 291726
Web: www.biddendenvineyards.com
E-mail: info@biddendenvineyards.co.uk

Owner and Winemaker: Julian Barnes

VINEYARD

First planted by the Barnes family in 1969, the vineyard is the oldest in the Southeast. 22 acres of south-facing slopes on sandy loam over weald clay. Most vines are trellised on Geneva Double Curtain and the main grape varieties are Ortega and Dornfelder.

WINERY

The capacity of the winery is 400,000 litres which caters also for cider production and private label apple juice.

WINES

Gribble Bridge Ortega Dry is the main seller; other wines are Huxelrebe, Ortega, Schonburger, Gribble Bridge Rosé, Biddenden Quality Sparkling Wine and Gribble Bridge Dornfelder. Biddenden is also the largest producer of traditional ciders and apple juice in Kent.

AWARDS

Past winners of the English Wine and Southeast Wines of the Year Competition. Kent Lifes' Best Vineyard 2004.

FACILITIES AND TOURS

Visitors are welcome to take a self guided tour of the vineyard and to a free tasting in the vineyard shop. Open 10am -5pm all year except Sundays in January and February. Guided Tours and meals are available subject to advance booking.

SALES

Wine sales are mainly through the vineyard shop and via the website. Cider and Apple Juice can be found in many retail outlets across the Southeast.

DIRECTIONS

From Biddenden take the A262 towards Tenterden. After 1½ miles turn right on to the Benenden road. Take the next left and the vineyards will be found after 150 metres.

BOOKERS VINEYARD LTD

BOOKERS VINEYARD LTD
Foxhole Lane, Bolney,
West Sussex RH1 5NB
Telephone: 01444 881575
Website: www.bookersvineyard.co.uk
Email: sam@bookersvineyard.co.uk

Owners: Mr & Mrs R. Pratt and Mrs S. Linter
Winemaker: Mrs S. Linter

VINEYARD

Originally established in 1973 with 3 acres, the vineyard has expanded to 23 acres on south and south-western facing slopes on a sandstone and clay soil.

VARIETIES

The pre-dominant grape varieties are Rondo, Pinot Noir, Chardonnay and Pinot Gris.

WINERY

A brand-new 400 square metre winery has just been built with state-of-the-art equipment including specialist red wine fermenters to ensure consistent exposure of the fermenting juice to the grape skins.

WINES

The main brands are Dark Harvest red, Autumn Spice white and Barts Bubbly a traditional-method sparkling rosé.

AWARDS

Recent awards include a bronze medal in the International Wines and Spirits Competition for Dark Harvest 2001 and a bronze medal also for Barts Bubbly Rosé 1995 in the same competition.

FACILITIES AND TOURS

The vineyard is open from 10.00am to 5.00pm from Monday to Saturday with tea/coffee and wines available in the wineshop. Pre-arranged group tours are welcome. Conference and function rooms are also available for up to 80 people.

SALES

Sales are mainly through the web-site or the vineyard shop. Please see the web site for details of other stockists and mail-order.

DIRECTIONS

Take the A272 west from the A23 at Bolney. Foxhole Lane is the second turning on the right.

CARR TAYLOR WINES LTD

CARR TAYLOR WINES LTD
Wheel Lane, Westfield,
Hastings East Sussex. TN35 4SG
Telephone: 01424 752501
Website: www.carr-taylor.co.uk
Email: sales@carr-taylor.co.uk

Owners: David and Linda Carr Taylor
Winemaker: Alex Carr Taylor

VINEYARD

8.5 hectares were first planted in 1971 on Geneva double-curtain trellis followed by a further 6.5 hectares in 1990. The vineyard slopes south-east on sandstone over wealden clay and ironstone, 45 metres above sea-level.

VARIETIES

A wide range of grape varieties is grown of which Reichensteiner and Schonburger are predominant.

WINERY

The winery was built in 1982 and has a capacity of 200,000 litres. It houses a 2 tonne pneumatic Willmes press and a 3 tonne Vaslin press. All sparkling wine is laid down for between 1 and 4 years before disgorging.

WINES

Carr Taylor were the first to produce sparkling wines commercially in England and continue to sell a wide range under their name – brut, vintage, non-vintage and rose. A range of still white and red wines are produced under the 'Vessel' and 1066 labels. Fruit wines, including Mead and Ginger Wine, are also made.

AWARDS

Recent awards include a gold medal in the 'Challenge International du Vin' for Vintage Sparkling 1996 and a bronze medal for '1066' in the International Wines and Spirits Competition. 70 awards have been won in the past 15 years.

FACILITIES AND TOURS

Visitors are welcome at the vineyard shop every day of the year (except Christmas and New Year), 10am - 5pm and to walk the vineyard trail. Groups and coaches are very welcome and should phone in advance.

SALES

Sales are mainly through the vineyard shop, telephone sales and the web-site. Please phone the vineyard for details of other stockists.

DIRECTIONS

From London, take the A21 to the outskirts of Hastings and pick up the brown tourist sign to the vineyard directing you to Westfield on the A28. At the Westfield crossroads turn left as directed by the tourist sign and the vineyard is 2/3rds of a mile on the left-hand side.

DENBIES WINE ESTATE

DENBIES WINE ESTATE
Denbies Wine Estate, London Road, Dorking,
Surrey RH5 6AA
Telephone: 01306 876616
Web: www.denbieswineestate.com

Owners: Mr & Mrs White and Family
Winemaker: Marcus Sharp

VINEYARD

Denbies Wine Estate is home to the largest vineyard in the UK and is one of the largest privately owned vineyards in Northern Europe. With 265 acres under vine, Denbies can produce up to 400,000 bottles from a good harvest. Denbies accounts for 10% (approximately) of all wine produced in the UK from 18 varieties of grape.

WINERY

The winery at Denbies uses a combination of traditional methods with modern equipment including stainless steel tanks, modern pneumatic presses and state of the art filters to create their fine wines.

WINES AND VARIETIES

The current range of wines have been divided into three categories: The Estate Range: Flint Valley (White - Seyval Blanc/Reichensteiner) and Surrey Gold (White - Muller/Bacchus/Ortega). The Cellarmasters Choice: Juniper Hill (White - Schonburger/Bacchus), Coopers Brook (White - Chardonnay Blend), Redlands (Red - Dornfelder/Pinot Noir), Rose Hill 2003 (Pinot Noir/Dornfelder). The Vineyard Select: Hillside Chardonnay (White – 100% Chardonnay), Yew Tree Pinot (Red - 100% Pinot Noir), Greenfield's Cuvee (Premium sparkling - Chardonnay/Pinot Meunier/ Pinot Noir).

WINE

The wines in these ranges have won many awards both nationally and internationally, including four awards in the International Wine Challenge 2003/2004. This year, Denbies have entered wines into the International Wine Challenge, International Wine and Spirit Competition and Decanter Wine Awards.

FACILITIES AND TOURS

The chateau-style visitor centre offers excellent facilities. Indoor "Wine Experience" tours operate all year including a film in the 360 degree cinema, a ride on the 'electric train' through the winery, followed by the tasting of 3 of Denbies wines. Denbies Wine Estate is located just off the A24, close to Dorking – Junction 9 off the M25. There are direct trains from London to Dorking station.

SALES

Selected wines are available from Sainsburys, Waitrose, Somerfield, Ocado and the P&O Ferry Line. The full range of wines are available from the Denbies shop, mail-order or online at www.denbiesvineyard.com

HEART OF ENGLAND

Welford Hill, Welford-on-Avon,
Warwickshire, CV37 8AE
Telephone: 07775 805806
Fax: 0709 2308223
E-mail: david@Heart-of-England.info
Web: www.Heart-of-England.info

Owners: David & Meryl Stanley
Winemakers: Owners and Martin Fowke (Owen Elias for Sonnet XVIII). Wines made off-site at Three Choirs.

VINEYARD

Well-managed and attractive, overlooking the Vale of Evesham on SW facing slopes with light sandy loam over gravel subsoil; local climate enjoys below average rainfall and above average sunshine, well suited to red wine varieties. First planted 3.5 acres in 1996; plans in hand to raise acreage from present 12 to around 20 acres. Given the rapid recognition of the first wines produced, this is a vineyard to watch for the future as the new production comes on stream.

VARIETIES

Phoenix, Seyval Blanc, Rondo, Triomphe d'Alsace, Regent, Pinot Noir, Pinot Gris, Pinot Blanc, Pinot Meunier, Fruhburgunder, Chardonnay, Ortega, Bacchus, Siegerrebe and plans for Madeleine Angevine.

FACILITIES AND TOURS

We welcome individual, discerning visitors with a 'Heart-of-England Experience' (tour, tutored tasting, video, dine with wines) and especially cater for groups of up to 30. All visits by appointment: please telephone or e-mail. Accommodation can be arranged locally. Only by appointment please.

WINES

National and Regional Prize winners '02 -'04 (UKVA President's trophy '03; MVA Attingham trophy '03; Regional Best Red '02, '03 and '04): Sparkling: Bolingbroke (Ch. Method); Whites: Festival (Med. Blend), Phoenix (Dry), Sonnet XVIII (Med), Arden Oak (barrel-aged); Reds: Othello (Blend), Oberon (Rondo, Triomphe) - Gold medal winner.

SALES

On/off licence; local wine-merchants; mail order through Website.

DIRECTIONS

Cross the river Avon at Welford, 3miles from Stratford on B439 to Bidford; go through village 0.7m up hill on far side. At top turn right, signed 'Welford Hill' - Vineyard at end of long drive.

ENGLISH WINES GROUP plc

ENGLISH WINES GROUP plc
Chapel Down Winery, Tenterden Vineyard,
Small Hythe, Tenterden, Kent. TN3O 7NG
Telephone: 01580 763033
Fax: 01580 765333
Web: www.englishwinesgroup.com
E-mail: sales@engishwinesgroup.com

Owners: English Wines Group plc.
Winemaker: Owen Elias. (Winemaker of the Year 2002 and 2003)

VINEYARD

First planted in 1977, Tenterden Vineyard covers 24.5 acres on Tunbridge Wells sandy loam. Substantial re-planting has taken place in recent years with Chardonnay, Pinot Blanc, Bacchus, Pinot Noir, Regent, Rondo and Dornfelder now being the main varieties. In addition,there are 180 acres of vines under contract across the South-East.

WINERY

The winery is the largest in England with a capacity of 1 million litres in temperature controlled stainless steel. All white and sparkling grapes are whole-bunch pressed and fermented by variety and vineyard. All sparkling wines are bottle fermented in the traditional method, spending between 9 months and 3 years on the lees before disgorging. Red wines are fermented in specialised fermenting tanks and usually spend some time in cask.

WINES

Quality Sparkling Wines under the Chapel Down brand include Chapel Down Brut NV, Chapel Down Vintage Brut, Chapel Down Pinot Reserve and Chapel Down Brut Rose. The Chapel Down range of blended and single varietal red, white and rose wines are produced from grape varieties including Bacchus, Pinot Blanc, Pinot Noir and Rondo.

AWARDS

Chapel Down Pinot Reserve 1999 was awarded a Gold medal in the 2004 International Wine Challenge. Bacchus and Pinot Blanc are consistent medal winners and feature in Matthew Jukes' Top 250 wines in the world. Curious Grape Pinot Noir 2002 was awarded a Gold Medal, Best Red Wine and Best Single Varietal Wine at the UKVA Awards 2004. At the UKVA Awards in 2003 and 2004, we were awarded 5 trophies, 3 gold medals, 17 silver medals and 20 bronze medals.

FACILITIES FOR VISITORS

Our visitor facilities have been completely refurbished and extended. The new 'Chapel Down Winery' opened at Easter 2005, is a spectacular operation as befits England's premier producer. Our wine and food shop sells the best wines in England plus a range of English cheeses, smoked meats, fish, pickles, preserves, confectionery and much more. The Bistro and Terrace offer excellent home-cooked food seven days a week in stunning surroundings. Our Herb Garden is a beautiful spot in which to relax; visitors can also stroll in the vineyards or take a guided tour of the winery – advance bookings only. Wine Tastings are always available. We also offer tailor-made tours and gift experiences for groups and individuals. **Call us for more information plus details of our conference and wedding facilities, special events, hampers and topiary courses.**

OPENINGS HOURS

Daily from 10.00am to 5.00pm throughout the year.

DIRECTIONS TO VINEYARD

From Tenterden High Street (A28) turn on to the B2082 at the traffic lights by the William Caxton pub. Follow the road for 2.5 miles to the sign for Small Hythe – the vineyard is a further 300 yards on the right. From Rye, follow the signs for Tenterden and the brown Vineyard signs on the B2082 for approx 8 miles.

SALES

Our wines are sold direct from the Vineyard shop, via our mail-order service and through our web-site. We supply major retailers including Waitrose and Booths, plus independent accounts including Hotel du Vin, Malmaison Hotels, Fortnum and Mason, The Savoy, The National Trust and Selfridges. Our wines are sold direct to the On and Off trade both in the U.K. and abroad.

LAMBERHURST VINEYARD

LAMBERHURST VINEYARD
The Down, Lamberhurst,
Kent TN3 8ER
Telephone: 01892 890412
Web: www. lamberhurstvineyards.co.uk
E-mail: info@lamberhurstvineyards.co.uk

Owners: Lamberhurst Estates Ltd
Vineyard Manager: Ian Button

VINEYARD

Lamberhurst is one of the best-known English vineyards having been established in 1972 and having played a leading role in the growth of English wines. The vineyard is on sandy clay loam and, unusually, faces north; although this means a slightly later harvest, it reduces the risk of early frost damage. Much of the total vineyard area of 17 acres has been re-planted recently with Bacchus, early Pinot Noir, Rondo, Regent and Ortega.

WINERY

Lamberhurst wines are now made at the Chapel Down winery at Tenterden.

FACILITIES AND TOURS

Lamberhurst Vineyard offers a wide range of attractions centred on the well-stocked vineyard shop and The Tasting Room Bistro. The shop sells a extensive range of award-winning English wines as well as an unusual English lager beer and the best of local ciders, fruit juices and fruit liqueurs. Wine tastings and guided tours are available on request. The Bistro offers fine wholesome food at exceptionally reasonable prices. A plant centre full of uncommon plant varieties, a beauty centre specialising in grape-seed oil skin treatment, and a Pet's Corner with pygmy goats all add to the attractions! The vineyard bar and restaurant – The Swan at the Vineyard – was voted one of the top 150 gastro pubs in the U.K. and has a superb reputation for an innovative and out-of-the-ordinary menu. Lamberhurst is an ideal setting for a conference, meeting, or celebration of any kind for up to 150 people. **Please contact us to see how we can assist you**.

DIRECTIONS

Coming from the North towards Lamberhurst village (A2l), at first roundabout turn right signposted Lamberhurst, follow road round then take a sharp right-hand fork sign-posted to Wadhurst (B2100). Turn right at the crossroads in 400 yards and pass the Swan at the Vineyard on the right. Opening hours: 10am-5.30pm

NEW HALL VINEYARDS

NEW HALL VINEYARDS
Chelmsford Road, Purleigh
Chelmsford, Essex, CM3 6PN
Telephone: 01621 828343
Web: www.newhallwines.co.uk
E-mail: newhall@newhallwines.co.uk

Owners: Mr P. W. Greenwood
Winemaker: Mr P. W. Greenwood

VINEYARD

Originally established in 1969, this 104 acre English Vineyard is one of the oldest and largest English wine producers in the country. The vines grown at New Hall have been planted on well-sheltered southern facing slopes of a shallow valley, which over the years has proved itself to have an almost ideal micro-climate for the growing of vines in England. Regularly produces above average crops of high quality grapes with naturally high sugars.

WINERY

Was first built in 1972 and since those days has been modernized with new stainless steel wine tanks, presses, and the latest wine making equipment to give it a capacity to process 25 tonnes of grapes a day and make just over 200,000 litres of wine a year.

WINES

Each year New Hall produces a range of different varietals, such as Bacchus, Huxelrebe, Pinot Noir, Pinot Gris, Ortega, Schonburger and a Sparkling Wine using a blend of Pinot Noir and Chardonnay. Many of these wines have won awards for quality in both English and European Wine competitions.

FACILITIES AND TOURS

The vineyard is open from 10.00 am to 5.00 pm from Monday to Friday and l0am until 1.30pm at weekends. Pre-arranged group tours are welcome between May and September for groups of up to 80 people.

SALES

Sales are mainly through the vineyard shop which is situated in the cellars under the 17th century farm house.

DIRECTIONS

From the A12 take the A414 towards Danbury and Maldon. Once past Danbury go straight across the next roundabout onto the B1010 and the Vineyard is 3 miles further down this road on the left.

NUTBOURNE VINEYARD

NUTBOURNE VINEYARD
Gay Street
Nr Pulborough
West Sussex RH20 2HH
Telephone: 01798 815196
Order on-line: wwwnutbournevineyards.com
Email: sales@nutbournevineyards.com

Owners: Bridget and Peter Gladwin

VINEYARD

The vineyard is situated on fertile green sand and has a good micro-climate being protected from prevailing winds by the South Downs. There are 18 acres in production.

VARIETIES

Six different grapes are grown namely Bacchus, Huxelrebe, Reichensteiner, Schonburger, Chardonnay and Pinot Noir. Total production can reach 50,000 bottles a year.

WINERY

The wines produced are made under the owner's supervision at Chapel Down, Tenterden. They include Sussex Reserve, which is a blend of grapes, Sussex Oak which is made of oak aged Huxelrebe and Bacchus as a single varietal. A Late Harvest Dry made of Schonburger and a traditionally made sparkling wine composed of Chardonnay, Pinot Noir and Reichensteiner are also produced. All wines are made to English Quality Wine standards.

AWARDS

A Bronze medal in the International Wine and Spirit Competition 2003.

FACILITIES AND TOURS

The vineyards are set in the grounds of Nutbourne Manor and visitors are invited to wander through the vineyards and to visit the lakes waterfalls and llamas. The vineyards is open from May to October from 2pm - 5pm on weekdays and 11am - 5pm on weekends and Bank Holidays.

SALES

The Windmill Shop sells a range of wines, and visitors are very welcome.

DIRECTIONS

Turn off the A29 near North Heath and follow signposts to Gay Street. The vineyard lies off the road from Gay Street to Nutbourne.

NYETIMBER VINEYARD

NYETIMBER VINEYARD
Gay Street, West Chiltington,
West Sussex RH20 2HH
Telephone: 01798 813989
Fax: 01798 815511
E-mail: info@nyetimber-vineyard.com

Owner: Andy Hill
Winemaker: Dermot Sugrue

VINEYARD

Nytimber was designed, planted and built specifically to make world-class sparkling wine to rival Champagne. The vineyard has a terroir similar to those in Champagne. It is level and the grapes grown are Chardonnay, Pinot Noir and Pinot Meunier. There are over 50 acres in production and all grapes are trellised on the single Guyot System identical to that used in the Champagne area. The estate was planted in 1992 by Americans Stuart and Sandy Moss, after a prolonged search for a site capable of rivalling the best estates in France.

WINERY

The custom built winery has been erected using current state of the art methods. The production methods indeed exceed the French rules including maturing the wines for at least 5 years - double the minimum required for champagne.

AWARDS

The vineyard has won countless awards since the first release of its Wines in 1996. It has won Gold Medals in international competition with the best champagnes. Most recently the vineyard won 4 of the 11 most prestigious trophies in the 2004 English and Welsh Wine of the Year Competition.

FACILITIES AND TOURS

This vineyard is not open to the public.

WINES AVAILABLE

The vineyard normally makes at least two sparkling wines, a 'Blanc de Blanc' (100% Chardonnay) and a 'Classic Cuvee' (a blend of Chardonnay, Pinot Noir, Pinot Meunier). Wines are stocked by Waitrose, Majestic and many fine wine merchants. Check the website for local stockists.

RIDGEVIEW WINE ESTATE

RIDGEVIEW WINE ESTATE
Fragbarrow Lane, Ditchling Common,
Sussex BN6 8TP
Telephone: 01444 241441
Fax: 01444 230757
E-mail: ridgeviewestate@aol.com
Web: www.ridgeview.co.uk

Owners: Michael and Christine Roberts
Winemakers: Michael and Simon Roberts

VINEYARD

The vineyard is situated on a low limestone ridge sloping south towards the South Downs. High hills keep the micro climate comparatively dry and positively hot in the summer.

WINERY

The winery produces about 55,000 bottles annually in a state of the art winery. The majority of the specialised equipment is imported from Epernay in Champagne. There is an underground cellar to store up to 250,000 bottles in perfect condition during the ageing process.

VINES

The vines comprise of Chardonnay, Pinot Noir and Pinot Meunier. Thirteen French clones on three different vine stocks ensure variety for blending. Trellising is traditional single guyot.

AWARDS

Since 2000 this vineyard has won 13 trophies and 42 medals in National and International competition including English Wine of the Year in 2000 and 2002 and 2 Silver Medals last year in France.

FACILITIES AND TOURS

The vineyard is open every day from 11am - 4.30pm for sales and tastings. Tours of the vineyard are £5 by appointment. There are also tutored tastings for groups which include blind tasting eight champagnes and sparkling wines. Ask what 'Merret' means!

CURRENT WINES

All wines are 'Cuvee Merret' with a range of styles from non-vintage Belgravia through rosé 'Fitzrovia' to a vintage 'Bloomsbury'.

SALES

The wines are available direct from Waitrose, Wine Society, Laytons, Sunday Times Wine Club and other speciality retailers or direct through the web-site.

DIRECTIONS

Fragbarrow Lane is on the left 1.1/2 miles north of Ditchling on the B2112 and the estate is about 1/4 mile down the lane.

THREE CHOIRS VINEYARD

THREE CHOIRS VINEYARD
Freepost SWC 3094 (for mail order)
Newent, Glos GL18 1LS
Telephone: 01531 890223
Fax: 01531 890877
E-mail: orders@threechoirs.freeserve.co.uk
Web: www.threechoirs.com

Owners: Three Choirs Vineyards Limited.
Winemaker: Martin Fowke

VINEYARD

75 acres makes this one of the larger vineyards, and shows what can be done, in England. First planted in 1975 (first vintage 1977). Soil: sandy free draining over local sandstone in a low rainfall corridor, average 20 inches pa. Trellising: Geneva double curtain. Foliar feeds but no pesticides are used. New vines are pot grown to save one year to maturity, and top grafting is being used after two years of trials.

WINERY

All stainless steel, temperature controlled, with warm room for red wines. French and American oak barriques. Winery improvements are paying dividends especially for red wines, but also for their wide range Quality still wines and sparkling white wines, which are their traditional mainstay.

VARIETIES

Bacchus, Siegerrebe, Phoenix, Seyval Blanc, Reichensteiner, Schonberger, Madeleine Angevine, Huxelrebe and reds: Rondo, Regent, Triomphe d'Alsace, Pinot Noir.

FACILITIES AND TOURS

Tastings, vineyard and winery tours are available, and the shop offers a wide range of local produce as well as the Estate's wines. There is a good (à la Carte) Restaurant (bookings required) and a small number of rooms are available for overnight stays, with an emphasis on comfort and quality. Pets are not encouraged. Three Choirs hope that visitors will come, see, enjoy and buy, with the emphasis on quality in every aspect of its activities. Open: 10-5 daily (shop); check web for tours/reservations/mail order.

WINES

Three ranges of wines are produced by Award-winning winemaker Martin Fowke – 'Premium Selection' provides entry level wines, 'Estate' is for the Trade (not supermarkets) and 'Cellar Door' is at the top end and only available from the winery shop. The aim is to produce wines for the public to drink and enjoy, rather than for competitions, although the wines have won numerous competitions and the prestigious VinExpo Gold Medal (1992).

SALES

From winery shop, mail order (contact by phone, fax or through web-site) and selected off-licences.

DIRECTIONS

From M50 take exit 3 and B4221 east to Newent. Take B4215 about two miles north from Newent and the vineyard is clearly visible on the east side of the road.

BARNSOLE VINEYARD

BARNSOLE VINEYARD
Fleming Road, Staple, Canterbury,
Kent CT3 2AF
Telephone: 01304 812530
Web: www.barnsole.co.uk
E-mail: vineyard@barnsole.co.uk

Owners: Dr. J.& Mr A Danilewicz
Winemaker: Dr John Danilewicz

VINEYARD AND WINERY

3 acres were first planted in 1993 on heavy loam over clay. Main grape varieties are Reichensteiner, Huxerebe and Rondo with some Regent and Fruhburgunder. Modern well-equipped winery with 13,500 litre capacity.

WINES

All current wines have achieved Quality Wine classification under the 'Canterbury Choice' label – Dry Reserve, Kent Classic, Pilgrims Harvest and Red Reserve and have won medals regularly in SEVA and UKVA Wine of the Year competitions.

FACILITIES AND TOURS

Open every day from 10.30 am to 5.30 pm (4.00 pm in winter). Admission and mini-tours are free. Full guided tours are also available.

DIRECTIONS

Refer to the web-site for detailed directions.

CHILFORD HALL VINEYARD

CHILFORD HALL VINEYARD
Chilford Hall, Linton,
Cambridge CB1 6LE
Telephone: 01223 895600
E-mail: simon@chilfordhall.co. uk

Owners: Chilford Hundred Ltd
Winemaker: Chris Durrant

VINEYARD

The 18 acre vineyard is planted on a south-west facing slope and includes, among other vines, Muller-Thurgau, Reichensteiner, Seigerrebe, Ortega and Schonburger. The winery has modern stainless steel tanks, a pneumatic press and some wines are oaked in barrel.

WINES

The vineyard produces fine wines, some oak fermented, including three white, one rose and one sparkling. They have regularly won national prizes. The wines are available through Corney & Barrow in Newmarket and at Cambridge Wine Merchants.

FACILITIES AND TOURS

The vineyard is open on Fridays, Saturdays, Sundays and Public Holidays from 1st March to 31st October. There are tastings, tours, a café and picnic area.

DANEBURY VINEYARDS

DANEBURY VINEYARDS
Nether Wallop
Stockbridge
Hants SO20 6JX
Telephone: 01264 781851
Fax: 01264782212
E-mail: patrick.westropp@danebury.com
Web: www.danebury com

Manager: Patrick Westropp
Winemaker: Vince Gower, Valley Vineyards, Twyford, Reading

VINEYARD

7 acres on chalk soil. The vines are 30% Auxerrois and Madeleine Angevine with 20% Bacchus, 15% Schonburger and 5% Rulander.

WINES

A range of white and sparkling wines is available.

FACILITIES AND TOURS

Vineyard and Cellar Tours, tastings, functions by appointment. 'A Taste of Hampshire', using our own wines, vegetables, fruits and herbs and locally produced meats, are very popular for groups of 14-25 people.

DAVENPORT VINEYARDS

DAVENPORT VINEYARDS
Limney Farm, Castle Hill,
Rotherfield, East Sussex. TN6 3RR
Telephone: 01892 852380
Web: www.davenportvineyards.co.uk
E-mail: info@davenportvineyards.co.uk

Proprietor and Winemaker: Will Davenport

VINEYARD AND WINERY

A 4 acre organic vineyard and well-equipped modern winery at Rotherfield and 8 acres at Horsmonden in Kent. Varieties grown include Pinot Noir, Auxerrois, Ortega, Huxelrebe, Bacchus, Siegerrebe and Faberrebe.All vines and winemaking have been Soil Association certified since 2000, and are managed without artificial fertilisers or pesticides.

WINES

Limney Estate bottle-fermented Quality Sparkling Wine 2001, Limney 'Horsmonden'dry white wine 2003. Wines are available for sale from the web-site. Free delivery to most mainland U.K. addresses. Also available from Vintage Roots (www.vintageroots.co.uk) and Vinceremos (www.vinceremos.co.uk)

TOURS

Visitors are welcome by appointment. Please contact the vineyard to arrange visits.

ICKWORTH VINEYARD

ICKWORTH VINEYARD
Ickworth House Park, Horringer,
Bury St Edmunds, Suffolk IP2 5QE
Telephone: 01359 251173
E-mail: macready@ickworthvineyard.freeserve. co.uk

Owners: Charles and Jillian Macready
Winemakers: White: Hans Schlieffer,
Red: Mary Mudd

VINEYARD

About 2.5 acres are planted in the old Walled Garden of Ickworth House. This is the only vineyard on a National Trust property. The trellising is the modern Scott Henry system and the grapes grown are Rondo, Bacchus, Auxerrois and Pinot Noir.

WINES

The red wines are made by Mary Mudd at Carters vineyard. White and sparkling wines are made by Hans Schlieffer at Frogs Alley Vineyard. The wines have won prizes in Regional competitions including the first ever gold medal for a red wine. The wines are largely sold at the National Trust shop and restaurant.

FACILITIES AND TOURS

The vineyard is open on the first Sunday of the month from June to October for self-guided tours and wine tastings.
Contact: Patrick Macready, 3, Wyken Cottages, Wykne Road, Stanton, Bury- St-Edmunds, Suffolk IP 31 2DW.

LEVENTHORPE VINEYARD

LEVENTHORPE VINEYARD
Bullerthorpe Lane,
Woodlesford Leeds,
Yorkshire LS26 8AF
Telephone: 0113 288 9088
Fax: 0113 266 7892
E-mail: janet@leventhorpevineyard.freeserve.co.uk

Owners: George* and Janet Bowden (*winemaker)

VINEYARD

5 acres (est. 1985), within Leeds City boundary, this is the most northerly commercial vineyard at present, but the local topography, south-facing slope and micro-climate are generous. Soil: sandy loam over sandstone. Mainly Madeleine Angevine, Seyval and (for reds) Triomphe. An interesting visit, given owners' knowledge and enthusiasm.

WINERY

Characterful West Yorkshire wines, made on site in small modern facility, have won many awards at regional level. Free tasting before purchase. Mainly white; limited amounts of sparkling and red wine.

SALES AND TOURS

Open: Sales 11-5 daily; Sun 12-4. Individual and group tours by appointment. At winery, local merchants and restaurants

LLANERCH VINEYARD

LLANERCH VINEYARD (CARIAD WINES)
Hensol, Pendoylan, Vale of Glamorgan,
Wales CF72 8GG
Telephone: 01443 225877
Fax: 01443 225546
E-mail: enquiries@llanerch-vineyard.co.uk
Web: www.llanerch-vineyard.co.uk

Owners: Peter and Diana Andrews
Winemaker: Martin Fowke, Diana Andrews
Open: Mar-Dec 10-5 daily

VINEYARD

7 acres planted 1986 – 1991. on sandy soils, with trellising to produce an open canopy. No pesticides and as chemical free as possible.

VARIETIES

Seyval Blanc, Bacchus, Kernling, Huxelrebe, Reichensteiner and Triomphe d'Alsace.

WINERY

Wine-making is now based at Three Choirs but uses own stainless steel equipment, with each variety separately fermented, and then blended.

FACILITIES AND TOURS

Shop/Coffee shop. Admission charge. Visitors can take unguided tours of the vineyard and woodlands; guided tours for groups of 20+ by arrangement. Children's play area. No pets. 10 rooms farmhouse B&B; 2 cottages, 2 apartments self-catering. A base for a short or long stay. (Own transport is necessary).

WINES

International and national award-winning 'Cariad' white, rosé and sparkling wines – notably the rosé and sparkling wines (IWSC bronze medal 2004), but also the whites, all of which reflect care and quality.

MUMFORDS VINEYARD

MUMFORDS VINEYARD
Shockerwick Lane, Bannerdown, Bath BA1 7LQ

Telephone: 01225 858367
Fax: 01225 852385
Web: www.mumfordsdvineyard.co.uk

VINEYARD

Mumfords is a family business two miles est of Bath in a beautiful setting in the Avon Valley. Four grape varieties are grown in 4 acres namely Madeleine Augevine, Kerner, Reichensteiner and Triomphe D'Alsace.

WINERY

The winery used modern stainless steel equipment to produce four white wines comprise a light crisp Madeleine Angevine and a full-bodied Kerner. The winery also produces a blended medium dry and a rose. The wines generally keep well for several years.

VISITORS

The vineyard and winery are open almost all year round and there are organised tours by arrangement. There is disabled access. All the wines may be tasted.

DIRECTIONS

At the mini-roundabout in Batheaston take the road to Colerne and after 1/2 mile follow the brown sign.

SHARPHAM VINEYARD

SHARPHAM VINEYARD
Sharpham Estate, Ashprington, Totnes,
Devon, TQ9 7UT.

Telephone: 01803 732203
Email: info@sharpham.com
Web: www.sharpham.com
Mail Order www.sharpham.com

Owner: Sharpham Partnership
Winemaker: Duncan Schwab

VINEYARD

A very picturesque vineyard of four hectares on south facing slopes on the bank of the River Dart. The grape varieties are: Madeleine Angevine, Kernling, Phoenix, Dornfelder and Pinot Noir.

WINERY

The winery is modern and produces a range of Red and White wines. Stainless steel tanks and oak barrels are used for fermentation and maturation.

PRIZES

Recent awards include Best English Red wine 2003. Awards for each of the 2003 wines at both the International Wine Challenge 2004 and English and Welsh wine Competition.

FACILITIES AND TOURS

A working farm with a small shop selling the wines and cheese which are also made on the estate. Self-guided walk and wine tasting, available daily for visitors – £3.60. On-licence, Disabled access, Free Parking. No coach access.

OPENING TIMES

Open March until Christmas Eve, Monday to Saturday 10am-5pm and Bank Holiday weekends and Sundays during June, July and August.

TITCHFIELD VINEYARD

TITCHFIELD VINEYARD
"Misty Haze", Brownwich Lane, Titchfield,
Hants PO14 4NZ
Telephone: 01329 845531
Fax: 01489 589250
E-mail: ca.baker@btclick.com
Web: www.titchfieldvineyard.com

Owners: Colin and Nicola Baker
Winemaker: Hans Schliefer

VINEYARD

Planted by the owners, this is a well managed operation. The vines grown include Seyval, Bacchus and Reichensteiner (each 15%). Madeleine Angevine, Auxerrois, Pinot Noir and Regent (each 10%) and three other red grapes. Production averages about 60hl in stainless steel variable capacity tanks and the wines are estate bottled. All the wines are sold locally in off-licences and restaurants. Red, white, sparkling and dessert wines are produced.

VISITORS

Only by special arrangement. Obtain detailed instructions if arranging a visit

AWARDS

Wessex Vineyard Association Gold Medal for red wine – Pinot Noir.

WROXETER ROMAN VINEYARD

WROXETER ROMAN VINEYARD
Wroxeter,
Shrewsbury,
Shropshire SY4 6PQ
Telephone: 01743 761888
Fax: 01743 761400
Web: www.wroxetervineyard.co.uk

Open: 10-5 daily; Sun 11.30-5.
Owners: Christine, David* & Martin* Millington (*winemakers).

VINEYARD

9 acres on a sheltered sandy plateau protected by local hills, adjacent to Roman ruins of Uriconium (Wroxeter). The main varieties are Dornfelder, Rondo, Regent, Regner, Madeleine Angevine, Reichensteiner and Phoenix.

WINERY

Modern s/steel, pneumatic presses etc. and own labs. Traditional methods used for Regional award-winning red and white blends, single varietals and sparkling wines - suitable for vegetarians.

FACILITIES

Shop, café, tours, tastings, self-catering vineyard lodges caravan field, and small 5 van site. 'Vineyard experience': an entertaining and informative introduction.

SALES

At winery shop and mail order via web.

DIRECTORY

a'Becketts Vineyard
High Street, Littleton Parnell, Devizes, Wiltshire SN10 4EN
Tel: 01380 818153 Fax: 01380 816669
Website: www.abecketts.co.uk
Email: abecketts.co.uk@aol.com
Owners: Lynn and Paul Langham
Producers of still white and red wines, located in mid Wiltshire halfway between Avebury and Stonehenge.

Brightwell Vineyard
Rush Court, Shillingford Road, Wallingford,
Oxon OX10 8LJ
Tel: 01491 836586 Fax: 01491 832354
Email: wines@brightvines.freeserve.co.uk
Website: www.brightwines.co.uk
Proprietors: Carol and Bob Neilson
Visits and tastings by appointment. Award winning white and red wines from 14 acre vineyard.

Carter's Vineyard
Green Lane, Boxted Colchester, Essex CO4 5TS
Tel: 01206 271136   Fax: 01206 273625
Email: enquiries@cartersvineyards.co.uk
Website: www.cartersvineyards.co.uk
Contact: Ben Bunting
A range of still and sparkling wine produced in their winery powered by wind and sun generated energy.

Coach House Vineyard
The Coach House, Salisbury Road, West Wellow, Hampshire SO51 6BW
Tel/Fax: 01794 323345
Email: roger.marchbank@btinternet.com
Proprietors: Roger and Margaret Marchbank
One of the five New Forest vineyards, Roger produces a single white wine from one acre.

Coddington Vineyard
Coddington, Ledbury, Herefordshire HR8 1JJ
Tel: 01531 640668
Email: denissavage@aol.com
Proprietors/winemaker: Ann and Denis Savage
Bacchus, Ortega and Pinot Gris vines. Produce sparkling, and still dry and medium dry white wines

Court Lane Vineyard
Ropley, Alresford, Hampshire SO24 0DE
Tel: 01962 773391
Email: courtlanewines@onetel.com
Proprietors/winemaker: Stephen Flook
Small vineyard of 0.6 ha established in 1978/9 with modern winery (1992). Producing award winning white wines. Vineyard and winery tours for small groups of up to about 20 by arrangement. Cellar door sales by the bottle.

Down St Mary Vineyard
Down St Mary, Crediton, Devon EX17 6EE
Tel: 01363 82300
Email: info@english-vineyard.co.uk
Website: www.english-vineyard.co.uk
Proprietors: Bernard and Penelop Doe
Winemakers: Vince Gower and Steven Brooksbank
A beautiful vineyard in the heart of mid Devon producing a sparkling wine and a range of still wines.

Manstree Wineyard
New Barn Farm, Shillingford St George, Exeter, Devon EX2 9QR
Tel: 01392 832218   Fax: 01392 8333712
Email: boyces@manstree.freeserve.co.uk
Website: www.boyces-manstree.co.uk
Contact: Tim and Simon Boyce
We produce a range of Still and Sparkling White Wines.

Parva Farm Vineyard
Parva Farm, Tintern, Chepstow, Monmouthsire NP16 6SQ
Tel: 01291 689636
Email: parvafarm@hotmail.com
Proprietors: Colin and Judith Dudley
In the beautiful Wye Valley, the vineyard planted in 1979 produces Quality sparkling and still white wines, rosé and red. Open to visitors all year.

Polmassick Vineyard
Polmassick Vineyard, St Ewe, St Austell,
Cornwall PL26 6HA
Tel/Fax: 01726 842239
Email: polmassick@btconnect.com
Winemaker: Barbara Musgrave
Cornwall's oldest vineyard. Estate produced dry and medium dry white, dry red, medium dry rosé and quality sparkling wines. Also Kea Plum and Strawberry wines from Cornish-grown fruit.

Purbeck Vineyard
Valley Road, Harmers Cross, Corfe Castle, Dorset BH20 5HU
Tel: 01929 481525
Email: michaelthorpe@purbeckwineyard.co.uk
Website: www.purbeckvineyard.co.uk
Proprietors: Michael and Sue Thorpe
Winemaker: Michael Thorpe
The three acre vineyard, established in 2000, is now producing its own red and white wines, with vineyard and winery tours becoming increasingly popular.

Sandhurst Vineyards
Hoads Farm, Crouch Lane, Sandhurst, Cranbrook, Kent TN18 5PA
Tel: 01580 850296
Email: ca.nicholas@btinternet.com
Website: www.sandhurstvineyards.co.uk
Contact: Anne Nicholas
Farm walk on mixed farm comprising wines, hops and sheep. Bed and breakfast accommodation available. Award winning wines for sale.

Somborne Vineyard
Frobisher Limited, Hoplands Estate, Kings Somborne, Nr Stockbridge, Hampshire SO20 6QH
Tel: 01794 388547 Fax: 01794 388701
Email: vickicook@frobisherltd.com

Welland Valley Vineyard
Welland Valley Vineyard, Marston Trussel, Market Harborough, Leics. LE16 9TX
Tel: 01858 434591
Email: welland@tiscali.co.uk
Website: www.wellandvalleyvineyard.co.uk
Proprietors: David and Jane Bates
Award winning sparkling, red, rosé and white wines. Sales and visits by appointment.

THE UK VINEYARDS ASSOCIATION

The UK Vineyards Association is formed from six Regional Associations and a grouping of the larger producers in the UK. It is the organisation to which grape growers and winemakers belong in order to share information, have a voice in Westminster and Brussels, and to promote their products. We welcome all who are interested in grape and wine production in the UK, large or small producers, and those who do not produce but who wish to be involved and informed.

For a small industry we have had a huge amount of media coverage in recent months, most of it full of enthusiasm, fuelled by the long summer of 2003. The St George's Day trade tasting is now firmly set as part of the Wine Trade Year and English Wine Week is part of the rural products year. The Wine of the Year Competition is our internal celebration of quality and success and the results list and award stickers bear witness to the consumer that our wines live up to expectation.

Recently a labelling system had to be developed to meet EU legislation introducing three official levels: Quality, Regional and Table Wine. This has become enshrined in UK legislation and is a working system with vineyards of all sizes having adopted it. The result is that there is a new confidence growing amongst wine makers that their wines can compete on quality with whatever the world sends to these shores, and there is a demand at prices that are realistic to production costs. An increasing number of wine drinkers in Britain are seeking out our wine.

This Guide to English & Welsh vineyards and wines has given our members the chance to be visible to a wide range of people with an interest in wine who wish to know more about the UK industry. If you have a mind to getting involved with vines and wines in the UK, please contact the UKVA office. We will do all that we can to help.

Roger Marchbank
UKVA Chairman
Email: roger.marchbank@talk21.com

REGIONAL ASSOCIATIONS

EAST ANGLIAN WINE GROWERS' ASSOCIATION

The East Anglian wine region, which now has its own officially recognised appellation, comprises Essex, Suffolk, Norfolk, Cambridgeshire and the Isle of Ely, Bedfordshire, Hertfordshire and North London. With its low rainfall, good sunshine record and suitable soils it was a successful wine growing area as long ago as Roman times. The Doomsday Book of 1086 recorded that 40 per cent of Britain's vineyards were to be found in this region.

Only a handful survived the Middle Ages, but in the past 40 years many modern vineyards have been planted, producing high quality grapes and award winning wines. Vine varieties like Bacchus and Muller Thurgau yield aromatic, fruity white wines. Madeleine Angevine, Reichensteiner, Huxelrebe, Ortega and Seyval are among other white varieties that have proved successful.

The development of new red grape varieties like Rondo, Regent and Acolon has resulted in increasing quantities of excellent red and rosé wine, and the noble but difficult Pinot Noir grape thrives in East Anglia. The best red wine in the 2004 English and Welsh Wine of the Year Competition was made from Pinot Noir grapes grown at East Anglia's New Hall vineyard.

East Anglian wines won eleven awards in that national contest. Three awards were for sparkling wines made by the traditional method, a category of rapidly growing importance and popularity.

The region holds its own East Anglian Wine of the Year Competition every June, with more than 60 wines being assessed in a blind tasting by an independent panel of distinguished judges.

Many of the region's vineyards are open to visitors, offering tours and free tasting (see map). There is a Wine Trail that takes in up to 16 vineyards, and wine lovers can buy a sample case of East Anglian wine at a discounted price after visiting any four.

The two-day Suffolk Show in Ipswich every summer presents another opportunity to compare these fine wines. All the wines on sale have taken part in a special competition. Seek out the trophy winners and compare them with their equally tempting rivals in the East Anglian wine marquee by the food hall.

The East Anglian Wine Growers' Association currently has 65 members. Membership is open not only to commercial growers but to anyone with an interest in the subject. Members are automatically enrolled also in the UK Vineyards Association. To provide a forum for discussion there are four general meetings each year, held at vineyards in different parts of the region. At each meeting a guest expert speaks on some aspect of vine growing or wine production. An enjoyable lunch follows this, giving members the pleasure of tasting and discussing one another's wines.

More details can be found on the Association's website:

Chairman
Piers Greenwood
New Hall Vineyard

EAST ANGLIAN WINE GROWERS' ASSOCIATION Continued

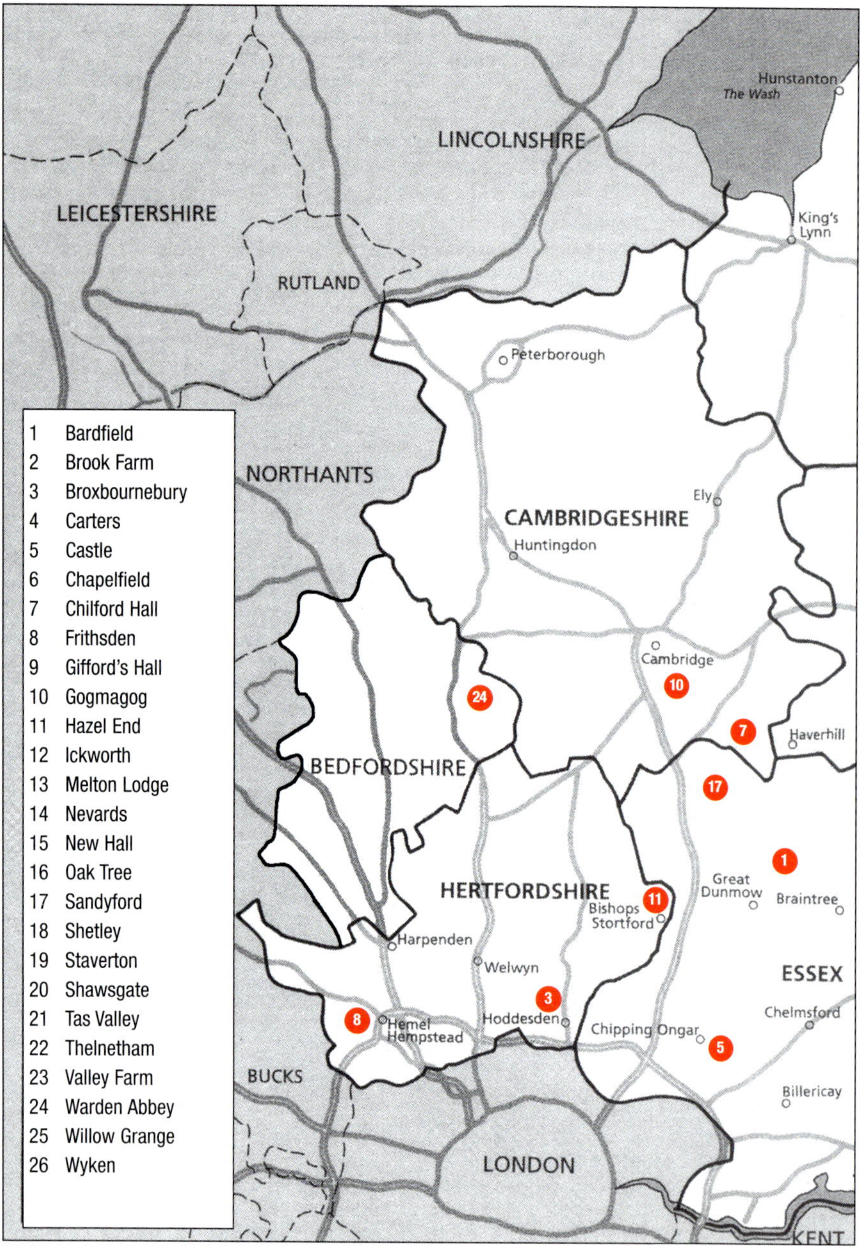

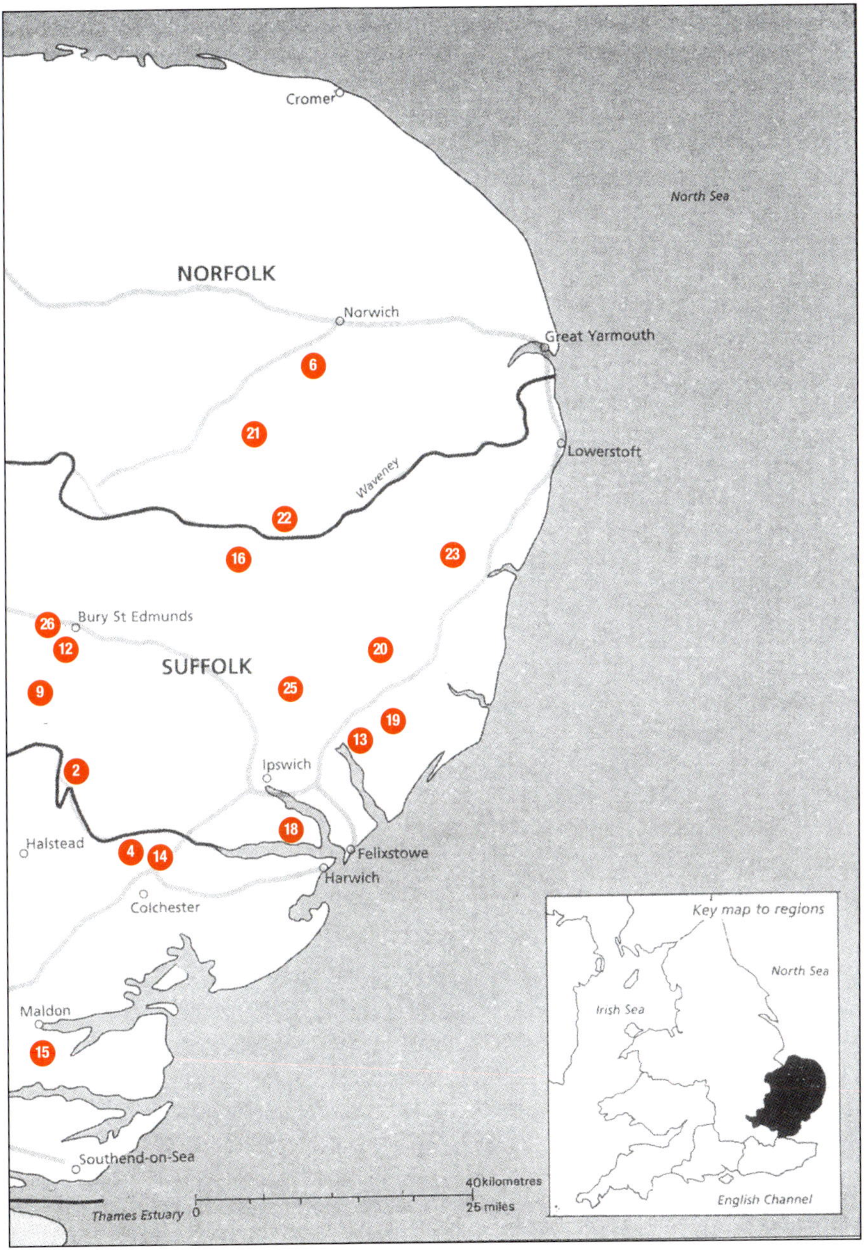

Cromer
North Sea
NORFOLK
Norwich
Great Yarmouth
6
21
Lowerstoft
Waveney
22
16
23
26
Bury St Edmunds
12
SUFFOLK
20
9
25
19
13
Ipswich
2
18
Halstead
4
14
Felixstowe
Harwich
Colchester
Maldon
15
Southend-on-Sea
Thames Estuary
0
40 kilometres
25 miles
Key map to regions
North Sea
Irish Sea
English Channel

Bardfield Vineyard
Great Lodge, Great Bardfield, Braintree, Essex CM7 4QD
Tel: 01371 810776

Brook Farm Vineyard
Brent Eleigh, Sudbury, Suffolk
Tel: 01787 248342

Broxbournebury Vineyard
Cock Lane, Hoddesden, Herts
Tel: 0208 886 2168

Carter's Vineyards
Green Lane, Boxted Colchester, Essex CO4 5TS
Tel: 01206 271136

Castle Vineyard
Vine House, Ongar, Essex CM5 9HF
Tel: 01277 364364

Chapelfield Vineyard
Pilgrim's Barn, Chapel Road, Spooner Row, Wymondham NR18 9LN
Tel: 01953 602749

Chilford Hall Vineyard
Chilford Hall, Linton, Cambridge CB1 6LE
Tel: 01223 895600

Frithsden Vineyard
Frithsden, Hemel Hempstead, Herts HP1 3DD
Tel: 01442 864732

Gifford's Hall Vineyard (Kemps Wine)
Hartest, Bury St Edmunds, Suffolk IP29 4EX
Tel: 01359 271497

Gogmagog Vineyard
The House on the Hill, Hinton Way, Great Shelford, Cambridge CB2 5AN
Tel: 01223 844075

Hazelend Vineyard
Hazel End Farm, Bishop's Stortford, Herts CM23 1HG
Tel: 01279 812377

Ickworth Vineyard
Ickworth House, Horringer, Bury St Edmunds, Suffolk
Tel: 01359 251173

Melton Lodge Vineyard
Melton Lodge, Melton, Woodbridge, Suffolk IP12 1LU
Tel: 0879 999 4404

Nevards Vineyard
Boxted Road, Boxted, Colchester, Essex
Tel: 01728 648471

New Hall Vineyards
Chelmsford Road, Purleigh, Chelmsford, Essex CM3 6PN
Tel: 01621 828343

Oak Tree Wines
Willow House, Fressingfield, Eye, Suffolk IP21 5PE
Tel: 01379 586868

Sandyford Vineyard
Salix Farm, Great Sampford, Saffron Walden, Essex CB10 2QE
Tel: 01799 586 586

Shawsgate Vineyard
Badingham Road, Framlingham, Suffolk IP13 9HZ
Tel: 01449 767067

Shotley Vineyard
Witenagemot, Frog's Alley, Below Church, Shotley, Ipswich IP9 1EP
Tel: 01473 787016

Staverton Vineyards
The Rookery, Eyke, Woodbridge, Suffolk IP12 2RR
Tel: 01394 460271

Tas Valley Vineyard
Hall Farm, Overwood Lane, Forncett St Peter, Norwich NR16 1LW
Tel: 01953 789445

Thelnetham Vineyard
Lodge Farm, Thelnetham, Diss, Norfolk IP22 1JL
Tel: 01379 890739

Valley Farm Vineyards
Wissett, Halesworth, Suffolk IP19 0JJ
Tel: 01986 785535

Warden Abbey Vineyard
Southill Park, Biggleswade, Beds SG18 9LJ
Tel: 01462 816226

Willow Grange Vineyard
Street Farm, Crowfield, Ipswich, Suffolk IP6 9SY
Tel: 01449 760612

Wyken Vineyards
Wyken Hall, Stanton, Bury St Edmunds, Suffolk IP31 2DW

PLEASE NOTE:
Some vineyards listed here may not be open to the public or may have restricted visiting hours. Please check by telephone before visiting to avoid disappointment,

SOUTH EAST VINEYARD ASSOCIATION

The South East of England has long been renowned for its fine fruit. The counties of Kent, East and West Sussex and Surrey have nearly half the national acreage of vineyards. We take our wine production and quality very seriously in the South East, and many of the finest wines are made here.

Being just 88 miles north of Champagne with almost identical geology and climate, it is not surprising that the South East is producing wines that rival, in blind tastings, the quintessential sparkling wine area – Champagne.

The combination of chalk and clay in the 'Downland' area of the South East bears an uncanny similarity to the Champagne region of France. Like them we also have a cool climate. Grapes for the finest, most complex wines are usually grown in cool climates.

"If someone wanted to make a Champagne look-alike, one of the most potentially successful sites would be in the counties of Kent and Sussex on the hills and slopes just ahove the English Channel." Oz Clarke

We have an annual competition judged by a panel of five judges, the majority of these being Masters of Wine. This enables us to have our wines judged to the highest standards.

The award ceremony is held at "the loveliest castle in the world", Leeds Castle in Maidstone, Kent. They also have a vineyard on site!

We also host 'The English Wine Festival' every year on the first weekend in September. This year to be held at 'The English Wine Centre', in Alfriston, East Sussex. It is definitely worth a visit to come and sample the some of best wines England has to offer.

We are a very successful region. We always welcome new members to our association including lay members. If you would like to find out more about wines from the South East or join our Association, we would love to hear from you. Contacts below:

SECRETARY
Mardi Roberts
c/o Ridgeview Wine Estate
Fragbarrow Lane
Ditchling Common
Sussex
BN6 8TP

Tel: 01444 241441
Email: ridgeview@aol.com

CHAIRMAN
Samantha Linter
c/o Bookers Vineyard Ltd
Foxhole Lane
Bolney
West Sussex
RH17 5NB

Tel: 01444 881575
Email: sam@bookersvineyard.co.uk

SOUTH EAST VINEYARDS ASSOCIATION

Continued

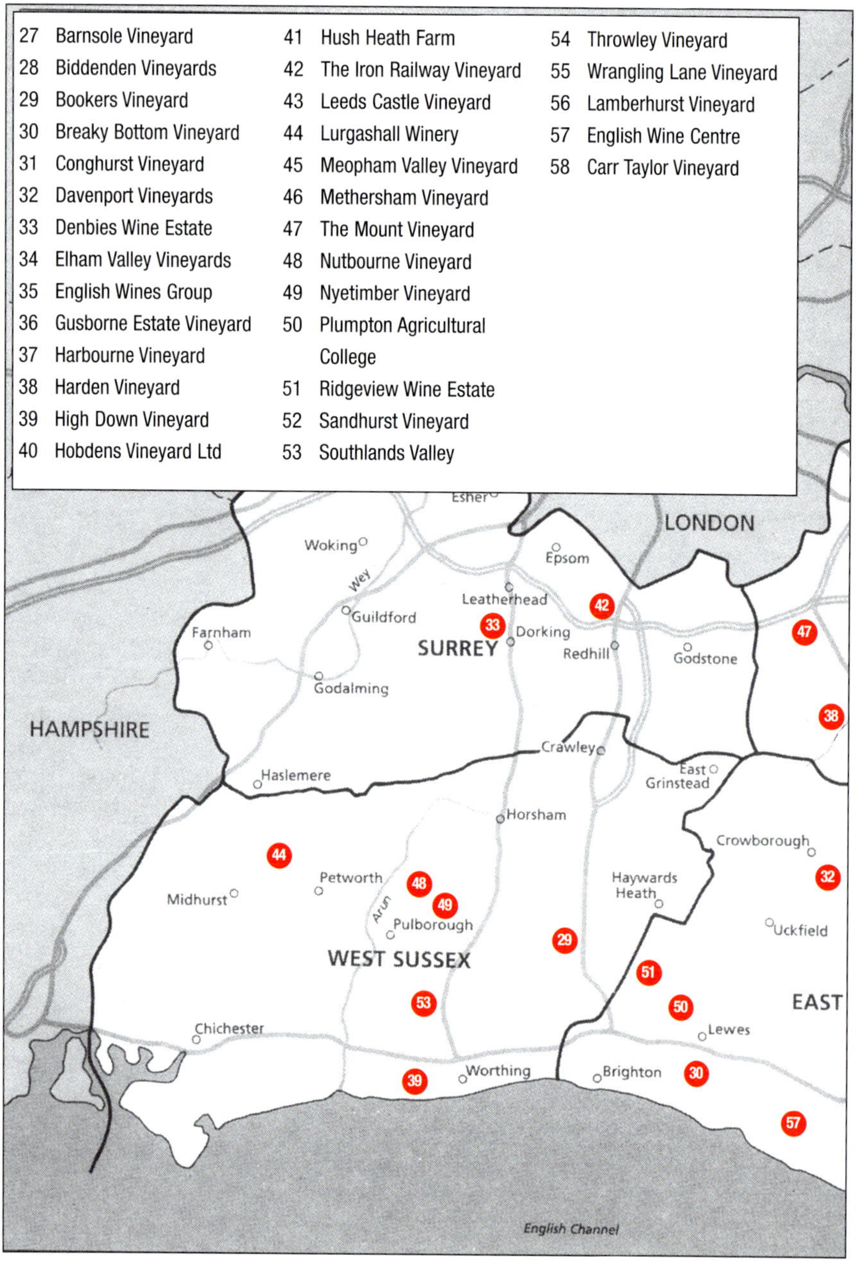

ESSEX
North Sea
Thames
Thames Estuary
Chatham
Rochester
45
Margate
Sittingbourne
Faversham
Ramsgate
Maidstone
Canterbury
Medway
43
54
27
Tonbridge
Deal
KENT
34
Tunbridge Wells
Ashford
28
Dover
56
Tenterden
Folkestone
41
37
Hawkhurst
35
31
52
36
40
Heathfield
Key map to regions
56
Rye
North Sea
SUSSEX
Irish Sea
Battle
58
Hastings
Eastbourne
English Channel
0
40kilometres
0
25 miles

Barnsole Vineyard
Dr. J. Danilewicz
Fleming Road, Staple, Canterbury, Kent CT3 1LG
Tel: 01304 812530

Biddenden Vineyards
Mr J. Barnes
Little Whatmans, Gribble Bridge Lane, Biddenden, Kent TN27 8DF
Tel: 01580 291726

Bookers Vineyard
Mr & Mrs R. Pratt
Foxhole Lane, Bolney, Haywards Heath, Sussex RH17 5NB
Tel: 01444 881 575

Breaky Bottom Vineyard
Mr P. Hall
Breaky Bottom, Rodmell, Lewes, East Sussex BN7 3EX
Tel: 01273 476427

Carr Taylor Vineyard
Mr A. Carr Taylor
Wheel Lane, Westfield, Hastings, East Sussex TN35 4SG
Tel: 01424 752501

Conghurst Vineyard
Miss J. Bridgwater
Conghurst Oast, Conghurst Lane, Hawkhurst, Cranbrook, Kent TN18 4RW
Tel: 01580 752634

Davenport Vineyards
Mr W. Davenport
Limney Farm, Castle Hill, Rotherfield, Crowborough, East Sussex TN63RR
Tel: 01892 852380

Denbies Wine Estate
Mr C. White
London Road, Dorking,Surrey RH5 6AA
Tel: 01306 876616

Elham Valley Vineyards
Mr N. Grant
Breach, Barham, Canterbury, Kent CT4 6LN
Tel: 01227 831266

English Wine Centre
Mr. C. Ann
Drusillas Corner, Polegate, East Sussex BN26 5QS
Tel: 01323 870164

English Wines Group
Mr O. Elias
Tenterden Vineyard Park, Small Hythe, Tenterden,
Kent TN30 7NG
Tel: 01580 763 033

Gusbourne Estate Vineyard
Mr A. Weeber
Griffin Farm, Appledore, Kent TN26 2BS
Tel: 01609 763008

Harbourne Vineyard
Mr L. Williams
Wittersham, Tenterden, Kent TN30 7NP
Tel: 01797 270420

Harden Vineyard
Mr R. Cole
Grove Road, Penshurst, Kent TN11 8DX
Tel: 01892 870221

High Down Vineyard
Mrs K. Hay
Littlehampton Road, Ferring, Worthing, West Sussex BN12 6PG
Tel: 01903 500663

Hobdens Vineyard Ltd
Mr & Mrs G. Fox
Hobdens, Wellbrook Hall, Mayfield, East Sussex, TN20 6HH

Hush Heath Farm
Mr R. Balfour-Lynn
Hush Heath Estate, Cranbrook, Kent TN17 2WG
Tel: 0207 479 2900

The Iron Railway Vineyard
Mr J. Russel Dicken
11 Vincent Road, Coulsdon, Surrey CR5 3DH
Tel: 01737 551829

Lamberhurst Vineyard
Mr I. Button
The Down, Lamberhurst,Kent TN3 8ER
Tel: 01892 890412

Leeds Castle Vineyard
Mr D. Horton
Leeds Castle, Broomfield, Maidstone, Kent ME17 1PL
Tel: 01622 765400

Lurgashall Winery
Prof J.P. Schooler
Lurgashall, Petworth, West Sussex GU28 9HA
Tel: 01428 707292

Meopham Valley Vineyard
Mr D. Grey
Norway House, Wrotham Road, Meopham, Kent DA13 0AU
Tel: 01474 812727

Methersham Vineyard
Mr P. Smith
Beckley, Rye, East Sussex TN31 6TX
Tel: 01797 260621

The Mount Vineyard
Mr J. Moulton
The Mount, Church Street, Shoreham, Sevenoaks, Kent TN14 7SD
Tel: 01959 524008

Nutbourne Vineyard
Mr P. Gladwin
Gay Street, Pulborough,West Sussex RH20 2HH
Tel: 01798 815196

Nyetimber Vineyard
Mr A. Hill
Gay Street, Pulborough,West Sussex RH20 2HH
Tel: 01798 813989

Plumpton Agricultural College
Mr J.C. Foss
Ditchling Road, Plumpton, Lewes, East Sussex BN7 3AE
Tel: 01273 890454

Ridgeview Wine Estate
Mr & Mrs M. Roberts
Upper Furzefield, Fragbarrow Lane, Ditchling Common, Hassocks, Sussex BN6 8TP
Tel: 01444 241441

Sandhurst Vineyard
Mr & Mrs C. Nicholas
Bourne Cottage, Bourne Lane, Sandhurst, Cranbrook, Kent TN18 5PA
Tel: 01580 850296

Southlands Valley
Mr J. Gilbert
Mitchbourne Farm, Malthouse Lane, Ashington, West Sussex RH20 3BU
Tel: 01903 892203

Throwley Vineyard
Mr D. Wilson
The Old Rectory, Throwley, Faversham, Kent ME13 0PF
Tel: 01795 890276

Wrangling Lane Vineyard
Mr R. Smith
c/o 33 Swan Close, Hatfield Peverel, Chelmsford, Essex CM3 2EN
Tel: 07967 585632

PLEASE NOTE:
Some vineyards listed here may not be open to the public or may have restricted visiting hours. Please check by telephone before visiting to avoid disappointment,

WESSEX VINEYARDS ASSOCIATION

The Wessex Vineyard Association covers the counties of Hampshire, Isle of Wight, Dorset and Wiltshire and has approaching 50 member vineyards, some commercially trading and open most days, while others sell wine through local shops.

Hampshire contains a larger number of the vineyards than the other counties but for 2005 we are seeing quite a large number of new plantings in Dorset and also a few in Wiltshire so we are looking forward to a wine renaissance here in Wessex.

Wessex can lay claim to being in at the start of the modern vineyard industry in the UK; back in the 1950's vineyards were planted at Hambleden in Hampshire and also by Lord Montagu of Beaulieu and they are still going strong today

Though we don't at present have as many large commercial vineyards as the south east of England, we can punch our weight and we have won prizes at National Competitions and also at our Annual Wessex Wine Competition.

Climate change, be that natural or aided by man, is having a positive effect on the development of vineyards. That allied to a clear approach to quality from the grape to the glass using the best wine-making techniques and some of the most modern wine-making equipment helps us produce wine that can take on established Old and New World contenders

Our Association welcomes new members and we have a range of activities across the year targeted at both people just interested in wine and also the professional grower; helping represent them at National and European Government levels. Please do contact me for more details.

Do explore the Wessex region, whether your interest is sparkling wine, white, red or dessert wines our vineyards have a good range of wines for sale and visiting a vineyard makes a great day out for all ages.

Enjoy!

CHAIRMAN WESSEX VINEYARDS ASSOCIATION
Paul Langham
High Street
Littleton Panell
Devizes
Wiltshire
SN10 4EN

Tel: 01380 816669
Email: abeckettswine@aol.com
Web: www.abeckettswine.co.uk

a'Becketts Vineyard
a'Becketts Farmhouse, High Street, Littleton Parnell, Devizes, Wiltshire SN10 4EN
Tel: 01380 818153

Adgestone Vineyard
Upper Road, Adgestone, Nr. Sandown, Isle of Wight PO36 0ES
Tel: 01983 402503

Beaulieu Vineyard
John Montagu Building, Beaulieu, Southampton, Hampshire SO42 7ZN
Tel: 01590 612345

Birchenwood Vineyard
Birchenwood Farm, Brook, Lyndhurst, Hampshire SO43 7JA
Tel: 02380 812595

Bishops Waltham Vineyard
Tangier Lane, Bishops Waltham, Hampshire SO32 1BU
Tel: 01489 896803

Charlton Barrow Vineyard
Charlton Barrow, Charlton Marshall, Dorset DT11 9DD
Tel: 01258 455533

Coach House Vineyard
The Coach House, Salisbury Road, West Wellow, Hampshire SO51 6BW
Tel: 01794 323345

Court Lane Vineyard
Court Lane, Ropley, Hampshire SO24 0DE
Tel: 01962 773391

Danebury Vineyards
Nether Wallop, Stockbridge, Hampshire SO20 6JX
Tel: 01264 781851

Doles Ash Farm Vineyard
Doles Ash Farm, Piddletrenthide, Dorset DT2 7RE
Tel: 01300 348248

Dunley Vineyard
The Hollies, Nr Whitchurch, Hampshire RG25 2TX
Tel: 01256 892613

Fonthill Glebe Wines
The Winery, Teffont Evias, Salisbury, Wiltshire SP3 5RG
Tel: 01722 716770

Horton Estate Vineyard
Horton, Wimborne, Dorset BH21 7JG
Tel: 01258 840258

Marlings Vineyard
Mead End Road, Sway, Hampshire SO41 6EE
Tel: 01590 681599

Merryhill Vineyard
Merry Hill Farm, Tanners Lane, East Wellow, Romsey, Hampshire SO51 6DP
Tel: 01794 512754

Northbrook Springs Vineyard
Beeches Hill, Bishops Waltham, Southampton, Hampshire SO32 1FB
Tel: 01489 892659

Priors Dean Vineyard
5 St Marys Road, Liss, GU33 7AH
Tel: 01730 894147

Purbeck Vineyard
Valley Road, Harmans Cross, Corfe Castle, Dorset BH20 5HU
Tel: 01929 481525

Rossiters Vineyard
Rossiters Farmhouse, Wellow, Isle of Wight PO41 0TE
Tel: 01983 261138

Setley Ridge Vineyard
Lymington Road, Brockenhurst, Hampshire SO42 7UF
Tel: 01590 822246

Continued

Somborne Valley Vineyard
Hoplands Farm, Kings Somborne, Stockbridge,
Hampshire SO20 6QH
Tel: 01794 388547

Sour Grapes Vineyard
Oak Tree House, Michelmersh, Romsey,
Hampshire SO51 0NQ
Tel: 01794 367300

Titchfield Vineyard
Misty Haze, Brownwitch Lane, Titchfield,
Hampshire PO14 4NZ
Tel: 01329 845531

Waterwynch Vineyard
Waterwynch, Itchen Abbas, Winchester,
Hampshire SO21 1AX
Tel: 01962 779229

Webb's Land Vineyard
Webb's Land, off Tanfield Lane, Wickham,
Hampshire PO17 5NS
Tel: 01329 833633

Wickham Vineyard
Botley Road, Shedfield, Southampton
SO32 2HL
Tel: 01329 834042

Winchester Vineyard
20 Arthur Road, Winchester, Hampshire
SO23 7EA
Tel: 01962 863492

Quoins Vineyard
Quoins, 32 Newtown, Bradford on Avon,
BA15 1NF
Tel: 01225 862334

Embley Wine
Jays Farm Vineyard, Embley Lane, East Wellow,
Hampshire SO51 6DN
Tel: 01794 511314

Wylye Valley Vineyard
Sutton End, Crockerton, Warminster, Wiltshire
BA12 8BB
Tel: 01985 211337

PLEASE NOTE:
Some vineyards listed here may not be open to the public or may have restricted visiting hours. Please check by telephone before visiting to avoid disappointment,

WESSEX VINEYARDS ASSOCIATION

Continued

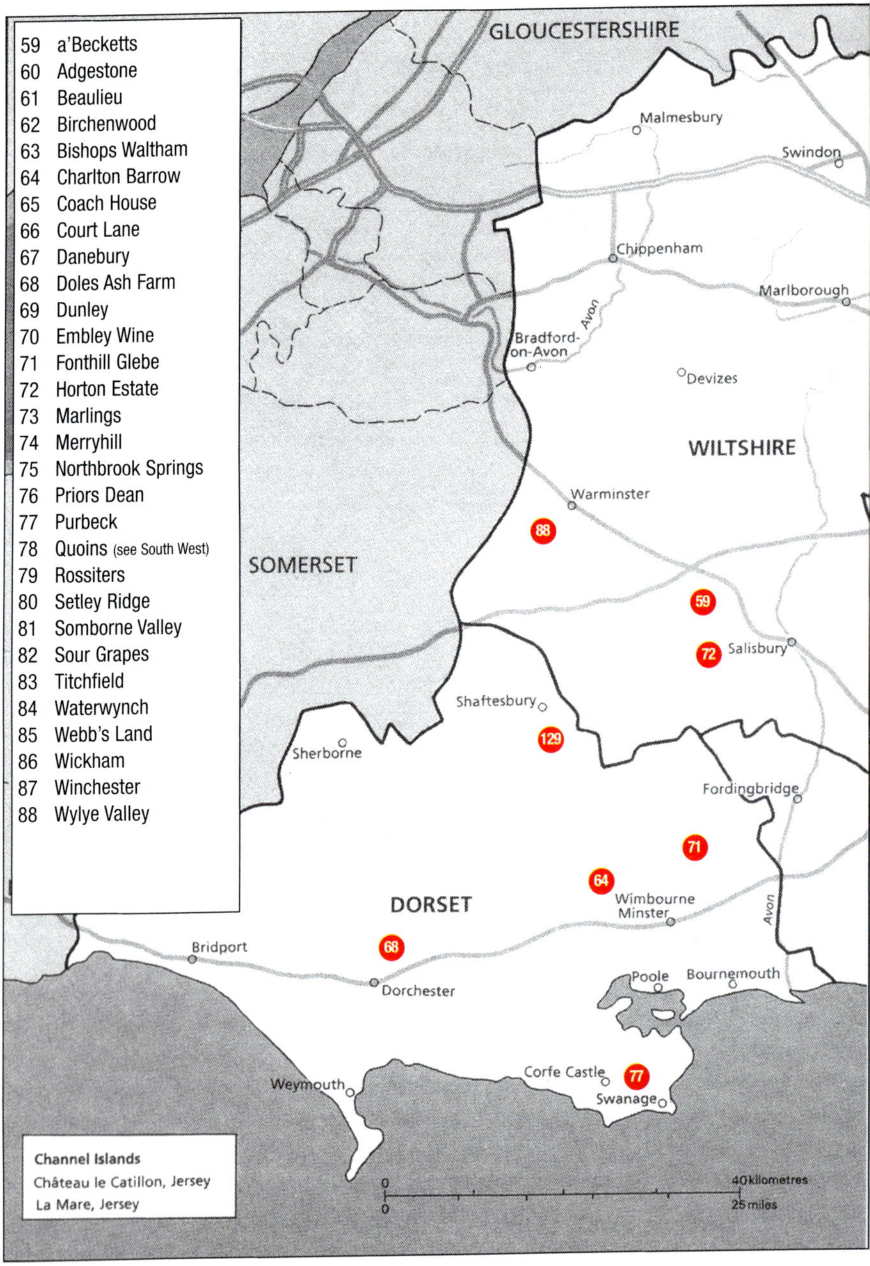

Key map to regions
North Sea
Irish Sea
English Channel
OXFORDSHIRE
BERKSHIRE
Thames
SURREY
Wey
Basingstoke
Whitchurch
69
Alton
67
Stockbridge
Winchester
84
Alresford
66
76
81
87
HAMPSHIRE
82
Petersfield
70
74
Romsey
65
63
Bishop's Waltham
Southampton
75
86
Wickham
WEST SUSSEX
85
62
Brockenhurst
Beaulieu
83
Fareham
80
61
73
Lymington
Cowes
Ryde
Yarmouth
Newport
79
ISLE OF WIGHT
60
Sandown
Shanklin
English Channel

SOUTH WEST VINEYARDS ASSOCIATION

The South West Vineyards Association aims to provide those in its region who have an interest in growing vines and making English, or Welsh, wines with a congenial, but not too formal, forum for sharing common interests.

The Association was founded by the pioneering vine grower and writer Gillian Pearkes who, starting with her own planting in the 1960's, soon attracted a keen following through her books, lectures and practical courses, becoming well known not just in Devon but throughout southern England.

Currently members are drawn not only from the South West peninsula but also from Wales, the Marches, around Bristol and down towards Wessex and, as can be seen from the regional map and list, they include many nationally famous vineyards.

The Association organises a number of events throughout the year, typically including a tasting and/or a guest speaker on a topic of interest. We hold our Annual Competition in September. This is nationally accredited and can award Regional quality status. We also publish a newsletter several times a year, giving notice of events to come and reporting on those which have taken place and other items of interest. Advertisements are included as a market place for members' wants and sales.

As the regional affiliate of the UKVA, we represent our members and participate in the essential work which can only be done at national level. We also act as a conduit for the distribution of information from the UKVA, including their informative 'Grape Press' journal, which contains essential regulatory information from Government Departments as well as other articles and listings of events. The UKVA's green 'pesticides' booklet is vitally important to commercial growers.

The Association seeks to publicise the industry regionally, and publishes a 'Visitor Leaflet' giving details of the vineyard visiting arrangements of those members who choose to join it.

For further information, please contact the secretary:

Martin Cursham
Burlands Farm
Staplegrove
Taunton
Somerset
TA2 6SN

Tel: 01823 452217
Fax: 01823 451726

Astley Vineyard
Jonty Daniels and Janet Baldwin
Astley, Stourport-on-Severn, Wors DY13 ORU
Tel: 01299 822907

Barras Moor Vineyard
Michael Chapman
Perrananworthal, Truro, Cornwall TR3 7PE
Tel: 01872 870237

Bryn Ceilog Vineyard
Ian D. Symonds
Fairfield, 14 Clinton Road, Penarth, Vale of Glamorgan CF64 3JB
Tel: 02920 711017

Camel Valley Wine
Bob, Annie and Sam Lindo
Little Denby Vineyard, Nanstallon, Bodmin, Cornwall PL30 5LG
Tel: 01208 77959

Coddington Vineyard
Drs Denis and Ann Savage
Ledbury, Herefordshire HR8 1JJ
Tel: 01531 640668

Down St Mary Vineyard
Penelope Cowell Doe and Bernard Doe
The Old Mill, Down St Mary, Crediton, Devon EX17 6EE
Tel: 01363 82300

Frome Valley Vineyard
David Longman
Paunton Court, Bishops Frome, Worcester WR6 5BJ
Tel: 01885 490736

Gelynis Fruit Farm & Vineyard
Roger Watt
Morganstown, Cardiff, City of Cardiff CF15 8LB
Tel: 02920 844440

Glyndwr Vineyard Ltd
Richard Norris
Glyndwr House, Llanblethian, Cowbridge, Vale of Glamorgan CF71 7JF
Tel: 01446 774564

Kenton Vineyard
Matthew Bernstein
Helwell Barton, Kenton, Exeter, Devon EX6 8NW
Tel: 01626 890367

Llanerch Vineyard
Peter and Diana Andrews
Hensol, Pendoylan, Vale of Galmorgan CF72 8GG
Tel: 01443 225877

Lulham Court Vineyard
Phil Pennington
Lulham Court, Madley, Hereford, Herefordshire HR2 9QJ
Tel: 01981 251107

Manstree Vineyard
Tim and Simon Boyce
New Barn Farm, Shillingford St George, Exeter, Devon EX2 9QR
Tel: 01392 832218

Monnow Valley Vineyards
Peter Baker
Great Osbaston Farm, Monmouth NP25 5DL
Tel: 01600 716209

Moorlynch Vineyard
Anne and Peter Farmer
Moorlinch, Nr Bridgwater, Somerset TA7 9DD
Tel: 01458 210393

Mumfords Vineyard
Tony and Margaret Cox
Shockerwick Lane, Bannerdown, Bath BA1 7LQ
Tel: 01225 858367

Oak Valley Wines
Paul Sibley
Bosue Farm, St Ewe, St Austell, Cornwall PL26 6EU
Tel: 01726 843159

Oatley Vineyard
Iain Awty
Cannington, Bridgwater, Somerset TA5 2NL
Tel: 01278 671340

SOUTH WEST VINEYARDS ASSOCIATION

Continued

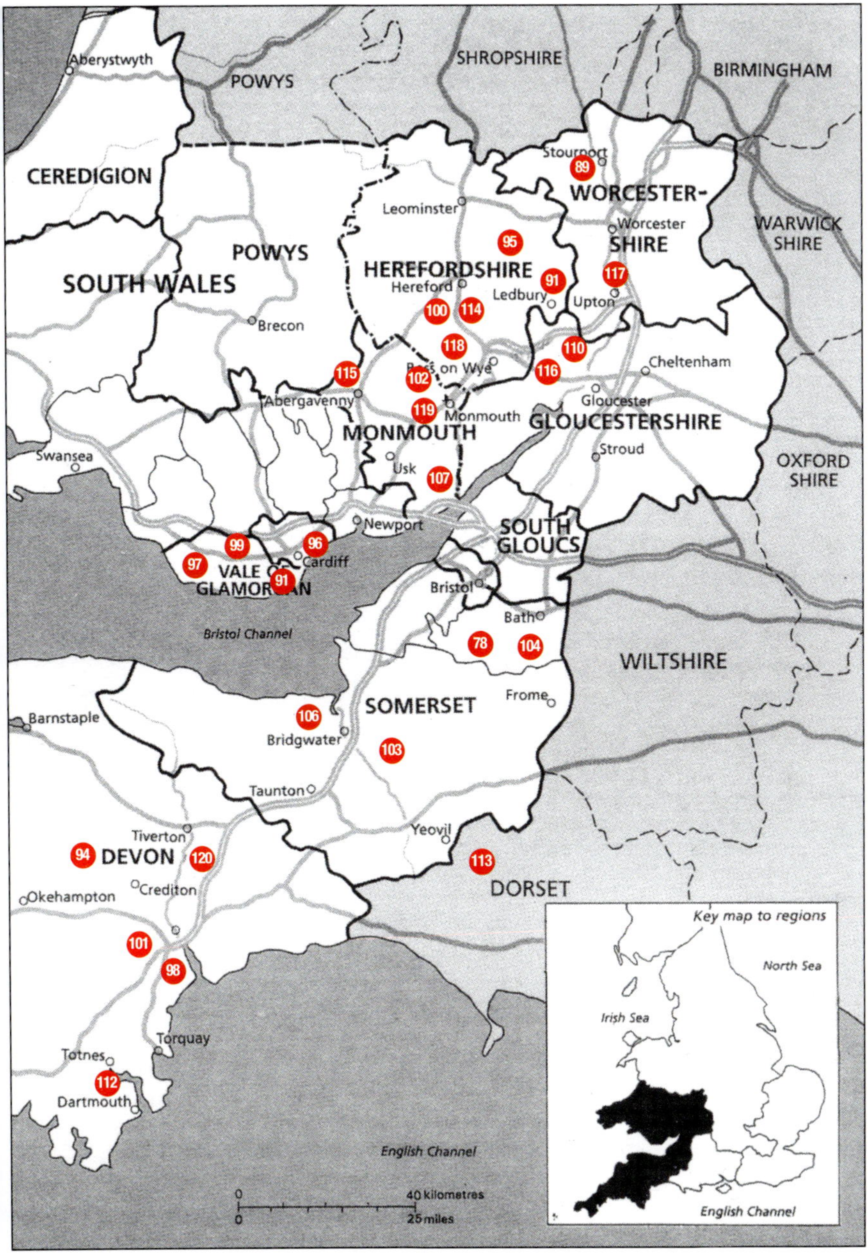
Aberystwyth
POWYS
SHROPSHIRE
BIRMINGHAM
CEREDIGION
Stourport
89
WORCESTER-
SHIRE
Worcester
Leominster
WARWICK
SHIRE
POWYS
95
HEREFORDSHIRE
SOUTH WALES
Hereford
91
117
Ledbury
Upton
100
114
Brecon
118
110
Ross on Wye
115
102
116
Cheltenham
Abergavenny
Gloucester
119
Monmouth
GLOUCESTERSHIRE
MONMOUTH
Stroud
Swansea
Usk
107
OXFORD
SHIRE
Newport
SOUTH
GLOUCS
99
96
97
Cardiff
VALE OF
GLAMORGAN
91
Bristol
Bath
Bristol Channel
78
104
WILTSHIRE
Frome
SOMERSET
Barnstaple
106
Bridgwater
103
Taunton
Tiverton
Yeovil
94
DEVON
120
113
DORSET
Crediton
Okehampton
101
98
Torquay
Totnes
112
Dartmouth
English Channel
0
40 kilometres
0
25 miles
Key map to regions
North Sea
Irish Sea
English Channel

Parva Farm Vineyard
Colin and Judith Dudley
Tintern, Chepstow, Monmouthshire NP16 6SQ
Tel: 01291 689636

Pemboa Vineyard
Lloyd Jones
Mellangoose Mill, Penboa, Helston, Cornwall
TR13 0QF
Tel: 01326 563116

Polmassick Vineyard
Barbara Musgrave
Polmassick, St Ewe, St Austell, Cornwall PL26 6HA
Tel: 01726 842239

St Anne's Vineyard
David Jenkins
Wain House, Oxenhall, Nr Newent,
Gloucestershire GL18 1RW
Tel: 01989 720313

St Martin's Vineyard & Winery
Graham Thomas
St Martin's, Isles of Scilly TR21 0QL
Tel: 01752 86019

Sharpham Vineyard
Mark Sharman with Duncan Schwab
Sharpham Estate, Ashprington, Totnes, Devon
TQ9 7UT
Tel: 01803 732203

Sherborne Castle Vineyard
J.K. Wingfield-Digby
Wake Court Farm, Bishops Caundle, Sherborne,
Dorset DT9 5NG
Tel: 01963 323249

Sparchall Farm
Edward Watkins
Tarrington, Hereford, Herefordshire HR1 4LE
Tel: 01432 850800

Sugar Loaf Vineyard
Louise Ryan
Dunmar Farm, Pentre Lane, Abergavenny,
Monmouthshire NP7 7LA
Tel: 01873 858675

Three Choirs Vineyard
Martin Fowke
Newent, Gloucestershire GL18 1LS
Tel: 01531 890223

Tiltridge Vineyard
Peter and Sandy Barker
Upper Hook Road, Upton on Severn, Worcs
WR8 0SA
Tel: 01648 592906

Treago Vineyard
Sir Richard Mynors
Treago, St Weonards, Herefordshire HR2 8QB
Tel: 01981 580208

Wernddu Wine and Vineyard
Frank and Leigh Strawford
Wernddu Farm, Pen-y-Clawdd, Monmouth
NP25 4BW
Tel: 01600 740104

Yearlstone Vineyards
Roger and Juliet White
Bickleigh, Tiverton, Devon EX16 8RL
Tel: 01884 855726

PLEASE NOTE:
Some vineyards listed here may not be open to the public or may have restricted visiting hours. Please check by telephone before visiting to avoid disappointment,

THE THAMES & CHILTERNS VINEYARDS ASSOCIATION

The T&CVA was formed in 1988 to further the interests of the vineyards, viticulturalists and winemakers in the area. Today the Association has over 100 members (including partners) spread between commercial vineyard owners, viticulturalists, winemakers and others with a general interest in viticulture and oenology. Some vineyards have their own wineries whilst others rely on contract producers and wine makers, including the internationally renowned John Worontschak. The grapes grown have been developed especially for northern climates and include Madeleine Angevine, the ever reliable Seyval Blanc, Reichensteiner and the red Triomphe and Dornfelder.

Our producers use these to make a range of crisp, fruity whites, interesting reds and prize-winning sparkling wines suitable for any discerning palate.

The Association has members residing in the counties of Berkshire, Bucklnghamshire, Dorset, Hampshire, Hertfordshire, Surrey, Wiltshire, Northamptonshire, Oxfordshire and Greater London. The Association holds three or four meetings and workshops per year on topics associated with viticulture and oenology and conducts an annual competition to find the best local wines. It also has a Non-Commercial Growers Group in which our non-commercial growers and winemakers can meet to discuss small-scale viticulture and vinification techniques. Members of this group include people with the intention to plant a vineyard, people with a few vines and others with several hundred vines.

The Association is affiliated to the United Kingdom Vineyards Association and Member vineyards regularly compete in national wine competitions (winning the UKVA English and Welsh Wine of the Year Competition no less than five times in seven years!). Association members receive both their own newsletter, the UKVA 'Grape Press' and other information from the UKVA.

For further information, membership details or newsletter subscriptions, please contact:

HONORARY SECRETARY
Sue Howlett
4 Privet Close
Lower Earley
Reading
RG6 4NY

Tel: 0118 921 0399
Email: sjhowlett@btopenworld.com

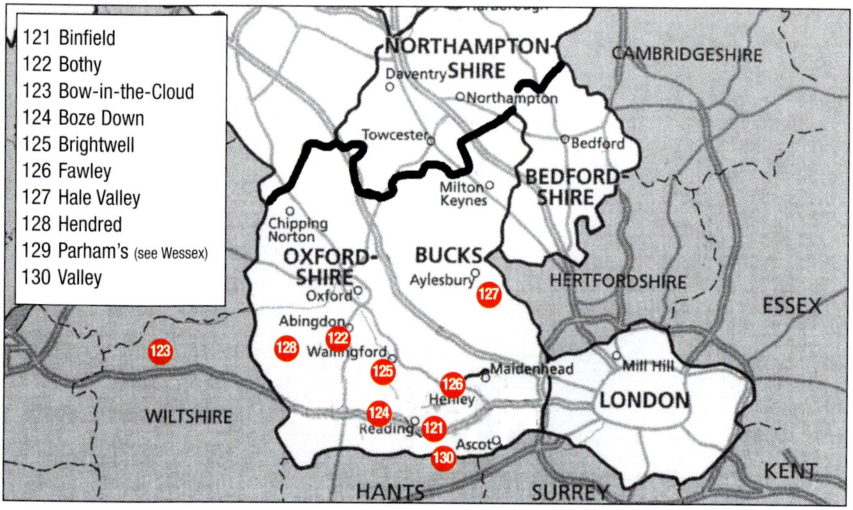

Binfield Vineyard
Mr & Mrs J. Hickey
Forest Road, Wokingham, Berkshire
Tel: 01344 305574

Bothy Vineyard
Mr & Mrs R. Liwicki
Frilford Heath, Abingdon, Oxon
Tel: 01235 868984

Bow-in-the-Cloud Vineyard
Mr K. Willingale
Noah's Ark, Garsdon, Walmesbury,Wilts
Tel: 01666 823040

Boze Down Vineyard
Mr & Mrs R.Conn
Hardwick Road, Whitchurch-on-Thames, Oxon
Tel: 0118 984 4031

Brightwell Vineyard
Mr & Mrs R. Neilsen
Rush Court, Wallingford, Oxon
Tel: 01491 836586

Fawley Vineyard
Mr & Mrs N. Sargent
The Old Forge, Fawley Green, Henley-on-Thames, Oxon
Tel: 01491 577998

Hale Valley Vineyard
Mr & Mrs A. Chapman
Boddington East, Hale Lane, Wendover, Bucks
Tel: 01296 623730

Hendred Vineyard
Mrs M. Mackinnon
Sheephouse Barn, Ludbridge, East Hendred, Oxon
Tel: 01235 833277

Parham's Vineyard
Mr & Mrs R. Phillips
Parham's Farm, Melbury Abbas, Shaftesbury, Dorset
Tel: 01747 853122

Valley Vineyards
Mr & Mrs P. Dart
Stanlake Park, Twyford, Berkshire
Tel: 0118 934 0176

PLEASE NOTE:
Some vineyards listed here may not be open to the public or may have restricted visiting hours. Please check by telephone before visiting to avoid disappointment,

MERCIAN VINEYARDS ASSOCIATION

The Association was founded in 1994 arising from the formation of the United Kingdom Vineyards Association. It was apparent, at that time, that a new Regional Association was needed to represent the increasing number of vineyards in the Midlands and North.

The name of the old Saxon Kingdom of Mercia was chosen to encompass all the different regions of our territory.

Currently there are over 60 members, from Anglesey to Lincolnshire and Gloucestershire to Scotland, reflecting the expanding boundaries of grape growing in the United Kingdom.

Meetings take place around the Region at least twice a year, usually with a speaker and an Annual Wine Competition is held in late August. Practical workshops are also held from time to time depending upon demand.

New members are always welcome whether they own a vineyard, are thinking of planting one, are interested in viticulture or merely learning more about English and Welsh wines. For further information or membership details please contact either the Chairman or Treasurer.

CHAIRMAN AND NEWSLETTER EDITOR

David Bates
Welland Valley Vineyard
Vine Lodge
Marston Trussell
Market Harborough
Leics
LEl6 9'IX

Tel: 01858 434591
Email: welland@tiscali.co.uk

TREASURER

Tony Skuriat
Eglantine Vineyard
Ash Lane
Costock
Loughborough
LE12 6UX

Tel: 01509 852386
Email: tony@skuriat.freeserve.co.uk

MERCIAN VINEYARDS ASSOCIATION

Continued

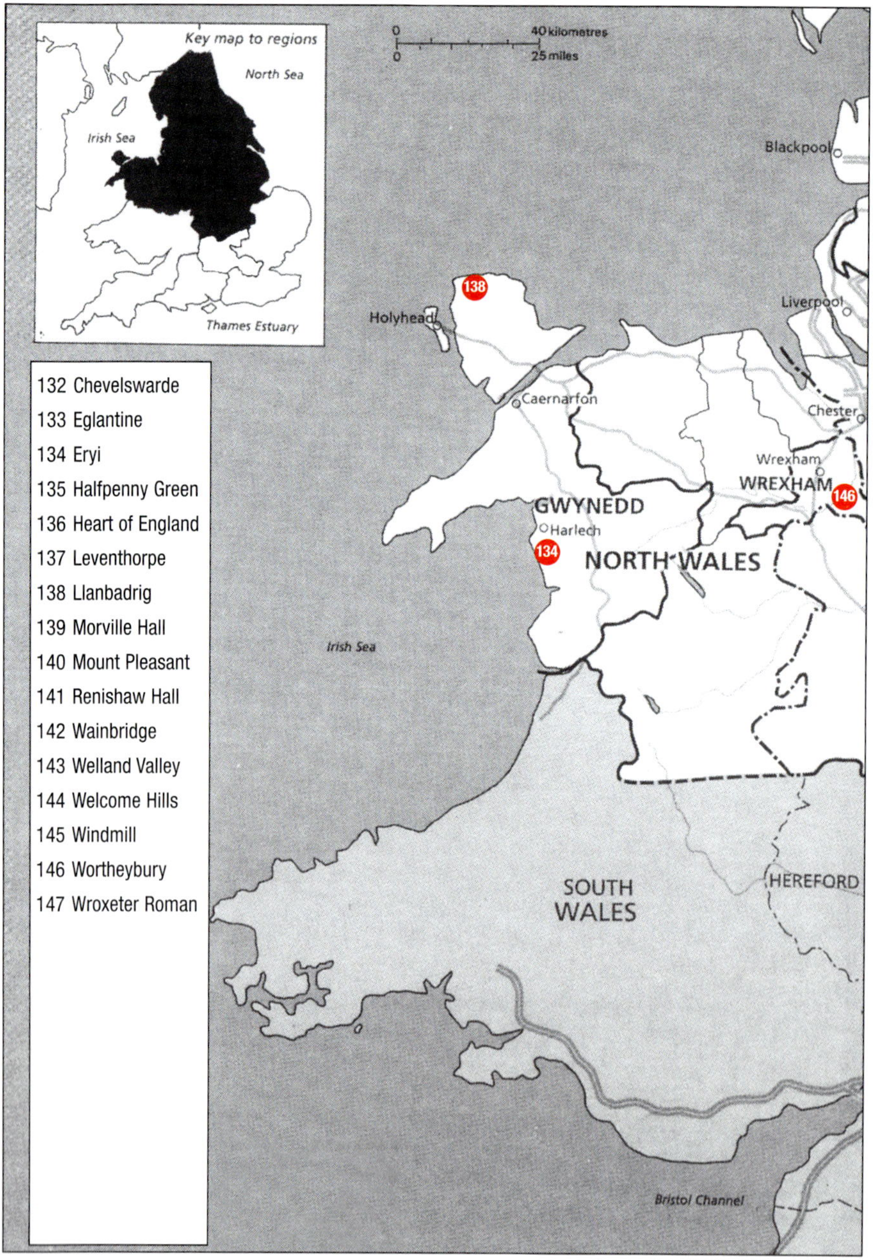

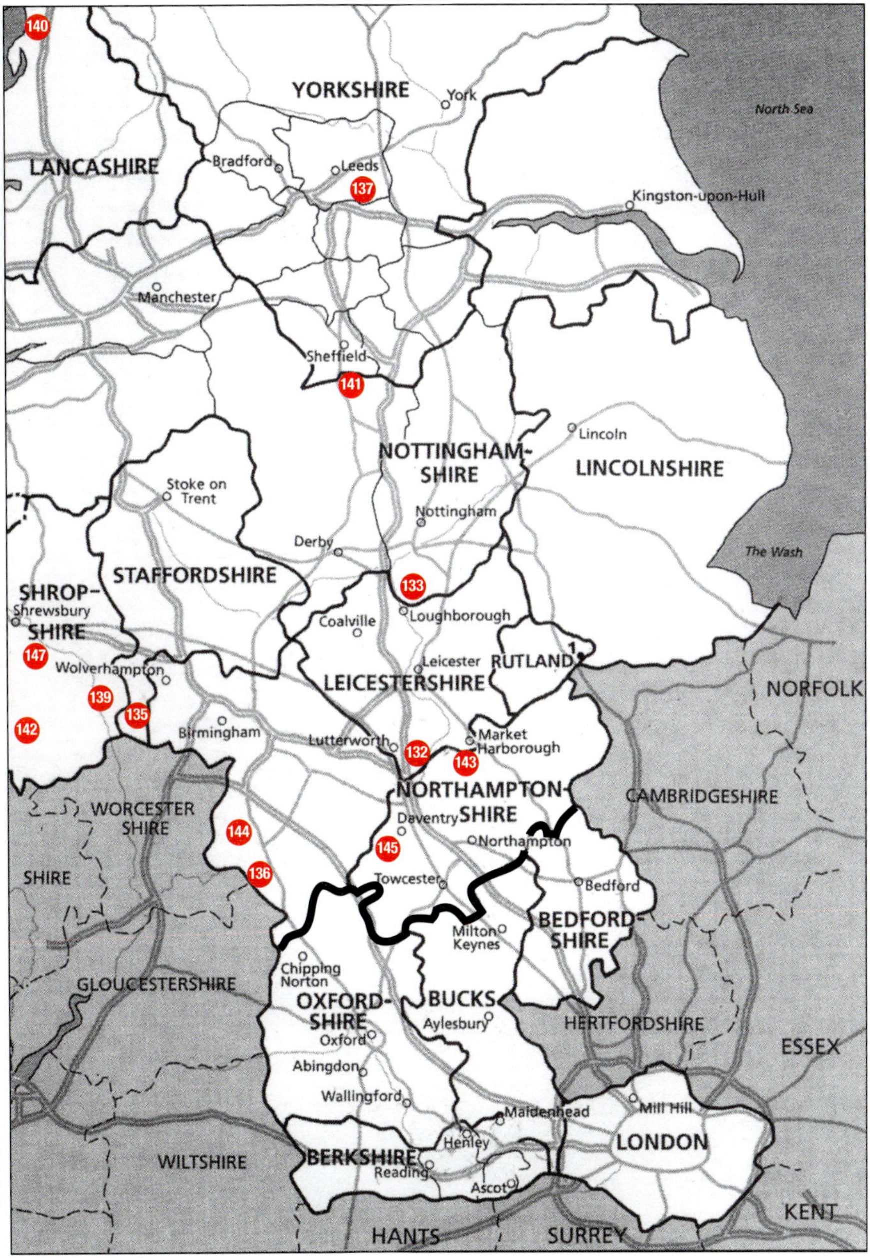
YORKSHIRE
York
North Sea
LANCASHIRE
Bradford
Leeds
Kingston-upon-Hull
Manchester
Sheffield
NOTTINGHAM-
SHIRE
Lincoln
LINCOLNSHIRE
Stoke on
Trent
Nottingham
Derby
The Wash
STAFFORDSHIRE
SHROP-
Shrewsbury
SHIRE
Coalville
Loughborough
Leicester
RUTLAND
LEICESTERSHIRE
NORFOLK
Wolverhampton
Birmingham
Lutterworth
Market
Harborough
NORTHAMPTON-
SHIRE
CAMBRIDGESHIRE
WORCESTER
SHIRE
Daventry
Northampton
SHIRE
Towcester
Bedford
BEDFORD-
SHIRE
Milton
Keynes
Chipping
Norton
GLOUCESTERSHIRE
OXFORD-
SHIRE
BUCKS
Aylesbury
HERTFORDSHIRE
Oxford
ESSEX
Abingdon
Wallingford
Maidenhead
Mill Hill
Henley
LONDON
WILTSHIRE
BERKSHIRE
Reading
Ascot
KENT
HANTS
SURREY
140
137
141
133
147
139
135
142
132
143
144
145
136
1

Chevelswarde Vineyard
Mr & Mrs J. Daltry
Chevel House, South Kilworth, Lutterworth, Leics. LE17 6DX
Tel: 01858 57530

Eglantine Vineyard
Mr & Mrs T. Skuriat
Ash Lane, Costock, Nr Loughborough, Notts, LE12 6UX
Tel: 01509 852386

Eryi Vineyard
Mr & Mrs D. Workman
Tay Artro, Llanbedr, Merioneth, Gwynedd, Wales LL45 2DZ
Tel: 01341 241251

Halfpenny Green Vineyard
Mr M. Vickers
Halfpenny Green, Bobbington, Staffs DY7 5EP
Tel: 01384 221122

Heart of England Vineyard
Mr & Mrs D. Stanley
Welford Hill Farm, Welford-on-Avon, Warwicks CV37 8AE
Tel: 01789 750565

Leventhorpe Vineyard
Mr & Mrs G. Bowden
Bullerthorpe Lane, Woodlesford, Leeds, West Yorkshire LS26 8AF
Tel: 0113 288 9088

Llanbadrig Vineyard
Mr & Mrs T. Barlow
Caeown, Camaes, Anglesey, Wales LL67 0LN
Tel: 01407 710416

Morville Hall Vineyard
Mr I. Rowe
Morvill Hall, Morville, Nr Bridgnorth, Shropshire WV16 5NB
Tel: 01746 714357

Mount Pleasant Vineyard
Mr & Mrs M. Graham
Mount Pleasant, Bolton Le Sands, Camforth, Lancs. LA5 8AD
Tel: 01524 732038

Renishaw Hall Vineyard
Sir Reresby Sitwell BT. DL.
Renishaw Hall, Renishaw, Nr Sheffield, Derbyshire S31 9WB

Wainbridge Vineyard
Mr & Mrs M. Hardingham
Wainbridge House, Clee St Margaret, Shropshire SY7 9DT
Tel: 01584 823543

Welcome Hills Vineyard
Mr & Mrs C. Gallimore
Vine Cottage, Kings Lane, Snitterfield, Stratford-upon-Avon, Warwicks CV37 0QB

Welland Valley Vineyard
Mr & Mrs D. Bates
Vine Lodge, Marston Trussel, Market Harborough, Leics. LE16 9TX
Tel: 01858 434591

Windmill Vineyard
Mrs D. Hiller
Windmill Hill Farm, Hellidon, Daventry, Northants NN11 8LG
Tel: 01327 262023

Worthenbury Vineyard
Mr & Mrs M. Seed
The Old Rectory, Worthenbury, Wrexham, North Wales LL13 0AW
Tel: 01948 770257

Wroxeter Roman Vineyard
Mr D. Millington
Wroxeter Court, Shrewsbury, Shropshire SY5 6PQ
Tel: 01743 761888

PLEASE NOTE:
Some vineyards listed here may not be open to the public or may have restricted visiting hours. Please check by telephone before visiting to avoid disappointment,

ENGLISH AND WELSH WINES ON THE UP AND UP

Julia Trustam Eve

The English and Welsh wine industry and its wines have probably undergone more change in recent years than any other wine producing country. English wines are more talked about, written about, and, importantly, available than ever before. It is purely and simply that English wines are now showing consistent quality, originality and value for money, and this has attracted the interest of wine writers and buyers alike.

The industry itself has been responding positively, by promoting its wines actively at every opportunity. Listeners to BBC's The Archers will be aware that there is a vineyard recently planted in Ambridge – a sure sign that the industry has been noted!

The UK wine industry last year celebrated fifty years since its first commercial harvest, and in a few short decades, no time at all by the standards of most wine regions, it has witnessed a very real change in attitude and in the professionalism of the winemakers. Producers are dedicated to the profitable production of competitive, good quality wines, whatever the weather. The weather is far less of a problem than people thought. There are few dramatic swings in production quantities year by year. The UK has produced on average 1.8 million bottles each and every one of the last 15 years save just 4 years when 2 were well down and 2 well above, and with improved winemaking, quality is also more consistent.

The attention of the national media was first drawn by the resounding success achieved by the sparkling wine producers against international competition. This country is able to produce wines as good as most Champagnes. There are also very exciting new styles of still white wines, which represent some 75% of all wine produced. New grape varieties are replacing some of the initial favourites and producing some wonderful results. Bacchus and Phoenix, for example, produce England's answer to Sauvignon Blanc. Red wines from the Pinot Noir grape have succeeded well in international competition and the attractively soft and fruity reds from the lesser-known but likeable Dornfelder and Rondo grape varieties are improving as more is known about them.

Without an extended history of winemaking tradition, this country's great advantage is to be able to offer something distinctly different, embracing the qualities found in the lesser-known varieties that thrive in the UK. There is now a greater feel for terroir and the grape varieties that suit our climate, and importantly how to get the best out of them. Intriguingly some of our best wines are rosé. Again they compare well with our continental and international competitors.

At the hub of all this is the talent that now exists in UK wine production. Winemaking in England now displays a understanding of the styles and flavours that can be successfully produced from English-grown grapes. Plumpton College in Sussex is to be commended for turning out most of our talented winemakers and vineyard managers through their dedicated wine studies courses. It is the only college of its kind in the UK. Many qualified students go on to gain some experience in other wine producing regions in the world, bringing back with them knowledge and experience.

ENGLISH AND WELSH WINES ON THE UP AND UP

Continued

After a gradual decrease in the area under vine, due to smaller and older properties closing down through retirement, there is now positive new growth in the industry. As demand increases we are expanding the industry to ensure a healthy production of English and Welsh wines year on year. Most popular grape varieties to be planted are the classic Champagne varieties Chardonnay, Pinot Noir and Pinot Meunier, and particularly in the South East, the Bacchus grape.

Another significant change is the accessibility to many vineyards across the country. Wine tourism is thriving in many corners of the UK – you do not need to cross the Channel to learn at first hand how wine is made, or of course to taste the results. Some 100 vineyards are open to the public in some shape or form. A number offer interesting and enjoyable days out and a truly memorable wine experience. The Quality Wine Scheme is a welcome change, giving our wines the same status and standards as are applied in the rest of Europe. You can taste the difference when you visit your local vineyard!

Most positive of all is that English and Welsh wines are now used and served in the highest circles. 2005 marks the Presidency of the UK of the European Union and G8. English and Welsh wines have been ordered in for serving during their tenure. Our wines are often served on official occasions by royalty and in Embassies and High Commissions throughout the world. It goes without saying that there are some sublime combinations to be found with some of the delicious and varied regional speciality food, which itself is witnessing a resurgence of interest.

There's a buzz in the air, and it is not of insects! With vineyards reporting record sales increases, and the prospects of a busy year ahead, the future for this industry is looking decidedly, bubbly, white, red and well – rosé!

APPELLATION

QUALITY WINE STANDARDS for ENGLISH AND WELSH WINES

(with acknowledgements to The Wine Standards Board)

Some years ago the U.K. wine production reached a size making it subject to European Commission rules. These rules are intended to give consumers some means of knowing which wines meet top international standards and which are of lesser quality. The idea is to create categories of wines similar, for instance, to the Appellation Controlée in France and the Denominazione di Origine Controllata in Italy. The highest category is called English (or Welsh) Vineyards Quality Wine.

The proposed regulations were not originally greeted with enthusiasm by smaller growers as they add additional cost. Many of them sold their wines locally and their clients were unlikely to be influenced by classification. Prior to 1991 the only classification was English (or Welsh) Table Wine, an uninspiring phrase of little significance.

The new standards are administered by DEFRA, who support a Quality Wine Committee with delegates from the United Kingdom Vineyards Association (UKVA), some expert advisers from the agriculture and food worlds and, finally, the Wine Standards Board (WSB), who enforce the rules created by the Committee based upon European Commission legislation. A two-part assessment of wines seeking Quality Wine status is administered by the Regional Industry Body (RIB) which, at the time of writing, is the UKVA.

Unmarked bottles of wine are sent to an independent laboratory for a vigorous chemical analysis, ensuring that no injurious chemicals are present in the wine, that it is sterile and has been properly treated to ensure it keeps in good condition for a reasonable time. Further unmarked bottles are sent to tasting panels, composed of 5 – 7 tasters that the RIB assembles at times during the year, in order to judge the acceptability of the wine in terms of colour, clarity, nose and taste, using a standardised marking system. Wines that receive pass marks from two-thirds of the tasters are declared as having passed.

However, before Quality Wine status can be granted, there are other criteria of provenance and production which also have to be met. For instance, only juice from certain recognised varieties of grape of the genus 'vitis vinifera' may be included in Quality Wine. There are also conditions as to alcohol content: this currently requires at least 6% alcohol from the natural sugars in the grapes, and a minimum actual alcohol content of 8.5%, whether or not the grape must was enriched by the addition of dry sucrose to augment the natural sugars in a poor harvest year. Inspectors from the WSB also check the vineyard and winemaking records to be certain that all winemaking processes have been properly and carefully carried out.

Only wines which meet all the requirements will be granted Quality Wine status – and a high international standard that is. Wines which fall short in some limited respects may nonetheless qualify as 'Regional Wines' (a superior table wine, akin to the French 'Vin de Pays') and some producers in highly identifiable regions are even preferring to adopt this standard instead of seeking Quality Wine status. Wines that do not meet Quality or Regional status may still be sold as 'Table Wine' with the designation United Kingdom.

The assurance of high standards introduced by the three categories of Quality, Regional and Table wines will be of enormous benefit to consumers and will, in consequence, be of significant and lasting benefit to the industry as a whole, and especially to those who are making major investment in improving quality and standards within their vineyards and wineries.

CURRENT WORLD TRENDS

Richard Bampfield, MW

Master of Wine Richard Bampfield has picked out eight trends in the international wine industry, each of which might impinge on English and Welsh wine producers.

Alcohol content:

With improvements in weather forecasting, the expansion of vineyards in warmer areas and better viticulture, many of the world's grapes are picked at higher levels of ripeness than was previously possible. This means that there is more sugar to be converted to alcohol and consequently alcohol levels in wines are rising. This trend does not suit everybody and may create opportunities for lower alcohol wines such as those from England and Wales.

Wine is commonly seen as one of the healthier alcohols, and lower alcohol wines are even healthier as they contain fewer calories. English wines should definitely appeal to the more weight-conscious among us!

Corks v. other closures:

There has been growing concern in recent years, especially in the UK, at the problems of taint being found in natural corks, leading to "corkiness" in wines. Many producers, particularly in New World countries, have started closing wine bottles with synthetic corks and, more recently, screwcaps. No single closure can yet claim to be the "perfect" closure for wine, but with many wines consumed within three years of production, and no tradition to follow, our producers can choose whatever proves best.

Container size:

Wine is literally sold in all shapes and sizes. In Ireland, the fastest growing sector of the market is the market for small, 18.75cl bottles of wine. In Scandinavia, they appear more ambitious (or maybe just more thirsty) because most wine is now sold in large, 3 litre wine boxes. What will prove best for English wine? Without any strong tradition, we are free to choose.

Cooler climate:

Wine producers in countries like Australia and California have realised that their hotter vineyards are all very well for producing large quantities of basic wine, but that high quality wine can only be produced in cooler vineyard sites. This is because grapes need a longer growing season in which to develop their aroma and flavour compounds. England, with its naturally cooler climate, should be well placed.

Variety:

Many people in the wine business claim membership of the ABC (Anything but Chardonnay) club, keen to ensure that we do not lose the great diversity of grape varieties grown around the world. If the market does tire of Chardonnay and seeks wines made from more unusual grape varieties, England, with its range of rarer grape varieties, will be well placed to capitalise.

Specialisation v. bulk:

In Brazil, they have discovered that certain vineyards can produce five grape harvests a year. England, with its one harvest a year, cannot compete with this, so it is just as well that the type of wine produced in England is so different from that produced in Brazil.

Vines need some water!:

In the warmer vineyards of the world, especially in Australia, water management for irrigation is becoming an increasingly crucial issue as underground supplies are declining. It hardly needs saying that England, with its plentiful rainfall, is spared this particular problem.

Wine tourism:

Wine tourism is booming in many parts of the world. In the Yarra and Hunter Valleys in Australia, Napa Valley in California and Stellenbosch in South Africa, many wine producers sell the bulk of their production directly from their cellars. As English wine grows, in both production and awareness, it must be hoped that the wine producers will be able to attract ever growing numbers of visitors to the vineyards and cellars.

RESEARCHING THE INTERFACE OF ROCK, VINE AND CLIME

HAS SCOTTISH WINE GOT A FUTURE?

Professor Richard C Selley

Senior Research Fellow, Imperial College, London, and author of 'The Winelands of Britain'

Geology has nothing to do with vinification, but much to do with viticulture. Geologists have studied the relationship between geology and viticulture for many years, with all the collateral conviviality that such demanding research necessarily entails. Vines grow on rocks of all types and of all ages, from the Precambrian granites of Portugal to the modem terrace gravels of the River Thames. *(Figure 1)* Superficially this suggests that geology has nothing to do with viticulture. Nothing could be further from the truth. The interplay of geology and climate controls the landscape within which a vineyard stands, and the soil in which it grows. Though vines grow on all rock types, geology exerts an important though indirect control on vine growth. The controls are principally related to topography and soil.

GEOLOGY AND LANDSCAPE

The grape vine, *vinis vitifera*, flourishes around the world where average temperatures are between 10-20°C. Where temperatures are optimal topography is of relatively little importance. Towards the polar limits of viticulture, however, topography becomes of increasing significance. In northern Europe, south-facing slopes allow increased solar radiation, especially in the autumn when grapes are ripening, In New Zealand, of course, north-facing slopes are to be preferred. On mid-summer day in southern England, for example, the angle of the sun is 62°, and a vineyard on a 30° slope will receive 8% more sunlight than one on level ground. This may not sound much, but by October, during the final days of grape ripening, the difference is 30%. Thus James Austin sagely remarked in 1813 'It is a truth universally acknowledged that an estate with a southerly prospect must be in want of a vineyard.' Topography is also important because slopes enhance drainage, headlands provide shelter, and topographically dammed valleys form frost hollows. Topography results from the interplay of geology and climatic processes, past and present.

GEOLOGY AND SOIL

The interplay of rock and climate also determines the soil in which a vineyard grows. Few vineyards are planted on bare bedrock; most are planted in superficial deposits derived from adjacent bedrock, but modified by climate. Thus many of the vineyards in sheltered valleys of the chalk downlands of southern England are actually planted in soils of glacial origin. Vines require moisture, but do not thrive in water-logged ground. Thus slopes are favoured, not only for enhanced sunlight, but also because they favour good drainage. Where vines lie above the water table the rock allows excess water to drain away so the roots do not become water-logged. But in dry summers the rootlets can penetrate the rock and extract moisture from the micro-pores of the rock itself. The importance of drainage and slope is demonstrated in *Figure 2* This shows how, for over 2 millennia, vineyards were planted on several different rock types, but always on well-drained south-facing slopes.

GEOLOGICAL PERIOD		ROCK FORMATION	VINEYARDS	
			BRITISH	MAINLAND
RECENT		Glacial, periglacial & alluvial superficial deposits	Morville Hall Thorncroft	
TERTIARY		Clays & sands	St Andrews Painshill Hale	Bordeaux
CRETACEOUS		Chalk	Adgestone Godstone Denbies Breaky Bottom Hambledon	Champagne
		Upper Greensand Gault Clay Lower Greensand Weald Clay Hastings Sands	Deepdene Purbeck Lamberthurst	
JURASSIC		Purbeck & Portland L-stns Kimmeridge Clay		
		M Jurassic L-stns		Burgundy
		Lias Clays		
TRIASSIC	NEW RED S-STN	Mercia mudstone Sherwood S-stn.		
PERMIAN		Sands Dolomites & shales		
CARBONIFEROUS		Coal Measures Main L-stn.	Wootton Pilton Eglantine	
DEVONIAN	OLD RED S-STN	S-stns & Shales	Three Choirs Sharpham Beenleigh Manor	Beaujolais Rhine & Moselle
SILURIAN ORDOVIAN CAMBRIAN PRECAMBRIAN		Assorted horrible igneous and metamorphic rocks	La Mare Grace Dieu	Muscadet Port

Figure 1. Stratigraphic section of the rocks in the British Isles and Euroland, showing how vines grow on rocks of many ages and types. This misleadingly suggests that geology has nothing to do with viticulture. (From Selley, 2004 © Petravin)

GEOLOGY AND CLIMATE

Vines evolved millions of years ago, and have grown wild in Britain for over 50 million years. During this period what is now northern Europe has enjoyed a tropical to sub-tropical humid climate. Only in the Ice Age of the last 2 million years have vines been absent during the glacial maxima, returning during warmer interglacial phases such as the present one. Recent research by the author has corroborated the Roman writer Saserna, who some 2000 years ago, argued that the vine could be used as an indicator of climate change. In Britain there are some 500 British vineyards, abandoned and extant dating from Roman to Modern times. Their distribution has been used to map the ebb and flow of vineyards across the British Isles over the last 2 millennia. *(Figure 3)* This advance and retreat of the vineyards across the British landscape correlates with changing temperature. In Roman times vineyards flourished SE of a line extending from the Humber to the Severn. Viticulture collapsed in the thermal Saxon sag, to be re-established in the Mediaeval Warm Period, extending nearly as far north as in Roman times, and advancing into south Wales. In the 'Little Ice Age' of the 15th-19th centuries, however, vineyards were restricted to southeast England. In the present Industrial Revolution Warm Phase vineyards have nearly reclaimed the former winelands of middle England and Wales.

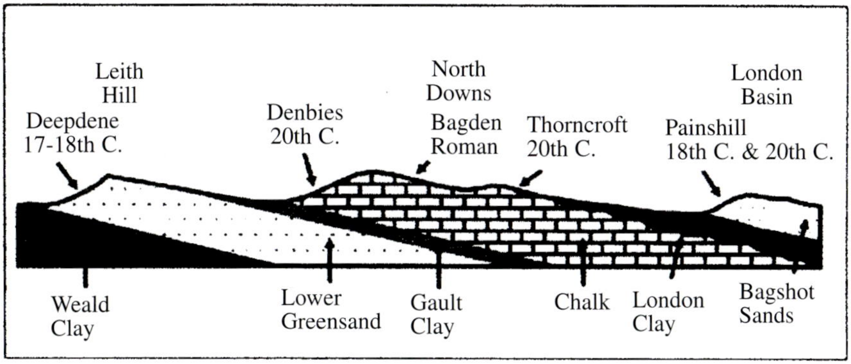

Figure 2. Geological south to north cross-section across southern England from the Weald to the Thames Valley showing how for 2000 years vineyards have been planted on rocks of many ages and types, but always on well-drained south-facing slopes. (From Selley, 2004 © Petravin)

Thus the figure shows the limit of Roman era vineyards and the retreat during the 'Little Ice Age'. Further it shows the expansion during the Industrial Revolution Warm Phase. But possibly its most interesting lines lie to the north. It is feasible that by 2050 we shall see vineyards on the southern slopes of the Lake District and the Derbyshire Peaks. By 2100 they may even extend up to the Great Glen of Scotland. Is it feasible to wean the Scots off whisky and onto their own home-grown wines? It will be tricky marketing!

All this and not a word about 'terroir'.

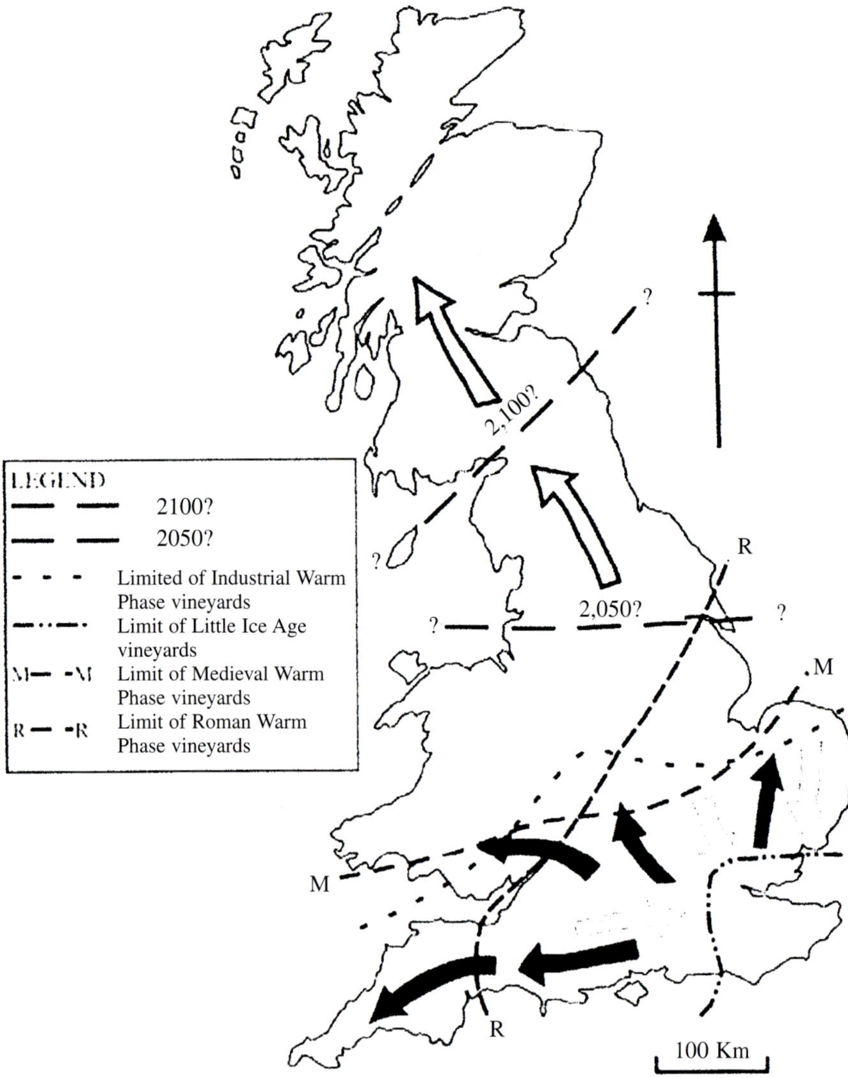

Figure 3. Map showing the northern and western limit of Roman, Medieval, Little Ice Age and Industrial Revolution Warm Phase vineyards. The delineates the ebb and flow of viticulture across the landscape correlative with climate change. Hypertentative northern limits of future viticulture dependant on the rate of global warming. (From Selley, 2004 © Petravin)

IT TAKES MORE THAN ENTHUSIASM

Colin Vaughan – ex-owner of Furnace Brook Vineyard

I came to the industry in 1989 with few preconceptions but with enthusiasm. I planted a small 3 acre vineyard and grew 4 varieties all of which ripened. So far so good! However, despite the vagaries of the weather, growing grapes was the least of my challenges. Making wine was a bigger challenge, marketing even more so.

I did not solve all the problems, but I gained some insights from being a member of a 14 vineyard strong co-operative, the first in the country and, like so many pioneering ventures, unprofitable. The co-operative grew vines in different locations, with at least 20 different grape varieties. We could not possibly market 20 different varietal wines, so we sought advice on wine making from Angela Muir M.W., whose skills are prized the world over.

Angela organised things in a commercial manner. Firstly she put the different grape varieties in groups with similar characteristics and specified how each group should be made. We used three different wineries, all operating on her instructions. On completion of the fermentation we had 12 large tanks at 3 wineries each made to different specifications. The next step was, to an amateur, quite astonishing.

I well remember spending a day collecting unmarked bottles of wines at the wineries in Surrey, Kent and Sussex, taking them to Angela and tasting them. On tasting them I did not like even one. Angela then got down to a little alchemy. She called it blending but it was magic to me! In 1994 she produced three wines using all our tanks with nothing wasted, each with very pleasing and different characters. Two continued improving for nearly 8 years! This was a massive lesson in the merits of vineyard co-operation, the use of highly skilled expertise, and of blending various wines (or assemblage).

Marketing was a different matter. We did not realise that, lacking a 'brand image' or even a vineyard shop it would be impossible to sell large quantities of wine quickly. One has to build up steadily but we clearly established that there is a market, and a big one.

Today there are a handful of large vineyards operating commercially. Their equipment and processes are modern, their staff well trained, and their products are good. Their prices are much more realistic and their marketing is effective.

There are over a hundred other commercial vineyards and many more smaller, private operations. All are bonded by an enthusiasm for what they do – and many cooperate at the winery stage, while retaining the individual characteristics of their terroirs. But not all of them, by any means, have the best grape clones or the ability to assemble quality wine regardless of the vintage – they can occasionally have spectacular successes, they can live in hope, but they will not make much money.

Enthusiasm has bought us to this point. It will continue to drive the business forward in countless ways. But, for longevity, the industry also needs professionalism in every aspect of winemaking, marketing and site selection, terroir or blending. Both have their place in a vibrant industry, but the emphasis has to be on quality not curiosity. For many I would suggest, the future will lie in cooperation, especially to achieve critical mass where new investment is needed, in modern wineries, or in marketing – in fact, in all those areas where enthusiasm alone cannot guarantee success.

That is the way forward, for the industry: but it still leaves plenty of room for the enthusiast to do his of her own thing. That is the freedom we all enjoy – that is the tradition of this fascinating industry. Long may it last!

WINE IS A MANY BLENDED THING

Dr Andrew M Shaw

Lecturer in Physical Chemistry

The chemistry of wine is complicated with perhaps half a million different compounds in every glass, changing over time during fermentation, ageing, oaking and even drinking. The volatile components leave the wine quickly either when stored or when heated on the tongue to give the floral bouquet and the crisp fresh taste of some English wines. The volatiles are all products of the sugar fermentation process started by the yeast. The vine, climate and soil contribute most to the sugar composition of the grape and provide the food for the yeast. Not all yeasts like the same sugars and different organisms produce different amounts of volatile compounds depending on the sugar supply.

The conversion of the grape sugars by the yeast naturally occurring in grape must, or those added by inoculation, is the point at which the chemical diversity of the blend increases. The sugars of the grape are essentially the food stuff of these organisms and these are converted into a rich diversity of volatile organic molecules of which ethanol is only one. The traditional brewers yeast (known technically as Saccharomyces cerevisiae) is not the first organism to start fermenting grape must. The early stages of fermentation in natural must are initiated by yeasts from the genera Hanseniaspora and Candida found naturally on the skin of the grapes. These early yeasts are much less hardy than the S. cerevisiae and are particularly sensitive to the ethanol composition. The growth of the early yeasts is rapid, stopping only when the ethanol concentration reaches 5% or so. The chemical diversity changes significantly however and test cultures with sequential mixes of Pichiafermentans for two days followed by S. cerevisiae show quantitative increases in the levels of acetaldehyde, ethyl acetate, propanol, other alcohols and glycerol. Longer fermentation with non-Sacc yeasts increases the volatile composition further.

The volatile organic compounds also assist with the colouring process. Most of nature's colours, from carrots to red cabbage, are fairly complex organic molecules that do not dissolve readily in water. However as the organic molecule content increases in the young wine, the colour compounds can be extracted from the skins of grapes or the oak of barrels to add colour to the wine in the later stages of fermentation. The tannins and phenolic compounds are now much happier in the solution than they would be in water and red wines in particular pick up their astringents, antioxidants and, in general, all of the compounds that affect the senses, so-called organoleptic compounds. Leaving white wine "sur lie" during or at the end of the fermentation process is an obvious example of organic extraction from both the pigments of the skins or the barrels. The process is most efficient when the full inventory of organic volatile molecules is present but this inventory changes with time.

Volatiles by their very nature will evaporate from the wine as it matures, lost to the atmosphere or to the barrels in which it is stored. The rate at which this happens depends on the temperature at which the wine is aged. As the volatiles disappear the extraction rate of pigments slows down but new chemistry starts. The larger molecules now in solution can change chemically by the process of oxidation and reactions initiated in the light, all of which are faster at higher temperatures producing more complex volatiles species. Too much oxidation and the alcohol oxidises to acid or vinegar. Analysis of the headspace above red wine as it breathes shows the variation in the composition and the sudden heating in the mouth of white wine releases the bouquet from the chilled state.

The magic blend of wine must be controlled throughout the production, whether by the nose of the master wine maker or the crude intervention of the scientist. Many possibilities present themselves: blend the grape must before fermentation to adjust the sugar and fermentation conditions; blend the yeasts with serial inoculation to change the volatiles inventory; blend the barrels at ageing and finally add the second set of volatiles in secondary fermentation for the sparkling wines. Science can help monitor the composition during the entire process, looking for a magic index for the perfect wine, but when all is said and done, it is the winemaker who must define the style of the wine he is creating.

INDEX

NOTES

NOTES

NOTES